America Today:
Observations and Reflections

William Archer

Contents

AMERICA TODAY:
OBSERVATIONS AND REFLECTIONS

BY

William Archer

LETTER I

The Straits of New York—When is a Ship not a Ship ? —Nationality of
Passengers—A Dream Realised.

R.M.S. *Lucania*.

THE Atlantic Ocean is geographically a misnomer, socially and politically a
dwindling superstition. That is the chief lesson one learns—and one has barely time
to take it in—between Queenstown and Sandy Hook. Ocean forsooth! this little
belt of blue water that we cross before we know where we are, at a single hop-skip-
and-jump! From north to south, perhaps, it may still count as an ocean; from east
to west we have narrowed it into a strait. Why, even for the seasick (and on this
point I speak with melancholy authority) the Atlantic has not half the terrors of the
Straits of Dover; comfort at sea being a question, not of the size of the waves, but of
the proportion between the size of the waves and the size of the ship. Our imagination is still beguiled by the fuss the world made over Columbus, whose exploit
was intellectually and morally rather than physically great. The map-makers, too,
throw dust in our eyes by their absurd figment of two " hemispheres," as though
Nature had sliced her orange in two, and held one half in either hand. We are slow
to realise, in fact, that time is the only true measure of space, and that London to-
day is nearer to New York than it was to Edinburgh a hundred and fifty years ago.
The essential facts of the case, as they at present stand, would come home much
more closely to the popular mind of both continents if we called this strip of sea the
Straits of New York, and classed our liners, not as the successors of Columbus's cara-
vels, but simply as what they are: giant ferry-boats plying with clockwork punctuality between the twin landing-stages of the English-speaking world.

Tomorrow we shall be in New York harbour; it seems but yesterday that we slipped out of the Cove of Cork. As I look at the chart on the companion staircase, where our daily runs are marked off, I feel the abject poverty of our verbs of speed. We have not rushed, or dashed, or hurtled along—these words do grave injustice to the majesty of our progress. I can think of nothing but the strides of some Titan, so vast as to beggar even the myth-making imagination. It is not seven-league, no, nor hundred-league boots that we wear—we do our 520, 509, 518, 530 knots at a stride. Nor is it to be imagined that we are anywhere near the limit of speed. Already the *Lucania's* record is threatened by the *Oceanic;* and the *Oceanic,* if she fulfils her promises, will only spur on some still swifter Titan to the emprise. [1] Then, again, it is hard to believe that the difficulties are insuperable which as yet prevent us from utilising, as a point of arrival and departure, that almost mid-Atlantic outpost of the younger world, Newfoundland—or at the least Nova Scotia. By this means the actual waterway between the two continents will be shortened by something like a third. What with the acceleration of the ferry-boats and the narrowing of the ferry, it is surely no visionary Jules Vernism to look forward to the time when one may set foot on American soil within, say, sixty-five hours of leaving the Liverpool landing-stage; supposing, that is to say, that steam navigation be not in the meantime superseded.

As yet, to be sure, the Atlantic possesses a certain strategic importance as a coal-consuming force. To contract its time-width we have to expand our coalbunkers ; and the ship which has crossed it in six days, be she ferry-boat or cruiser, is apt to arrive, as it were, a little out of breath. But even this drawback can scarcely be permanent. Science must presently achieve the storage of motive-power in some less bulky form than that of crude coal. Then

[1] The *Oceanic,* it appears, is designed to break the record in punctuality, not in speed. Nevertheless there are several indications that our engineers are not resting on their oars, but will presently put on another spurt. The very shortest Atlantic passage, I understand, has been made by a German ship. Surely England and America cannot long be content to leave the re-

cord for speed, of all things, in the hands of Germany.

the Atlantic will be as extinct, politically, as the Great Wall of China; or, rather, it will retain for America the abiding significance which the " silver streak " possesses for England—an effectual bulwark against aggression, but a highway to influence and world-moulding power.

Think of the time when the **Lucania** shall have fallen behind in the race, and shall be plying to Boston or Philadelphia, while larger and swifter hotelships shall put forth almost daily from Liverpool, Southampton, and New York! Think of the growth of intercourse which even the next ten years will probably bring, and the increase of mutual comprehension involved in it! Is it an illusion of mine, or do we not already observe in England, during the past year, a new interest and pride in our trans-Atlantic service, which now ranks close to the Navy in the popular affections ? It dates, I think, from those first days of the late war, when the **Paris** was vainly supposed to be in danger of capture by Spanish cruisers, and when all England was wishing her god-speed.

For my own taste, this sumptuous hotel-ship is rather too much of a hotel and too little of a ship. I resent the absolute exclusion of the passengers from even the most distant view of the propelling and guiding forces. Practically, the **Lucania** is a ship without a deck; and the deck is to the ship what the face is to the human being. The so-called promenade-deck is simply a long roofed balcony on either side of the hotel building. It is roofed by the "shade deck," which is rigidly reserved "for navigators only." There the true life of the ship goes on, and we are vouchsafed no glimpse of it. One is reminded of the Chinaman's description of a three-masted screw steamer with two funnels: "Thlee piecee bamboo, two piecee puff-puff, walk-along inside, no can see." Here the "walk-along," the motive power, is "inside " with a vengeance. I have not at this moment the remotest conception where the engine-room is, or where lies the descent to that Avernus. Not even the communicator-gong can be heard in the hotel. I have not set eyes on an engineer or a stoker, scarcely on a sailor. The captain I do not even know by sight. Occasionally an officer flits past, on his way up to or down from the " shade deck "; I regard him with awe, and guess reverently at his rank. The ship's company, as I know it, consists of the purser, the doctor, and the army of stewards and stewardesses. The roof of the promenade-deck weighs upon my brain. It shuts off the better half of the sky, the zenith. In order even to see the masts and funnels of the ship one has to go far forward or far aft and crane one's neck upward. Not a single human being have I ever descried on the " shade-deck" or on the towering bridge. The genii of the hundred-league boots remain not only inaccessible but invisible. The effect is inhuman, uncanny. All the luxury of the saloons and staterooms does not compensate for the lack of a frank, straightforward deck. The ***Lucania,*** in my eyes, has no individuality as a ship. It—I instinctively say "it," not "she "—is merely a rather low-roofed hotel, with sea-sickness superadded to all the comforts of home. But a first-rate hotel it is : the living good and plentiful, if not superfine, the service excellent, and the charges, all things considered, remarkably moderate.

What chiefly strikes one about the passengers is their homogeneity of race. Apart from a small (but influential) Semitic contingent, the whole body is thoroughly Anglo-Saxon in type. About half are British, I take it, and half American; but in most cases the nationality is to be distinguished only by accent, not by any characteristic of appearance or of demeanour. The strongly-marked Semites always excepted, there is not a man or woman among the saloon passengers who strikes me as a foreigner, a person of alien race. I do not feel my sympathies chill toward my very agreeable tablecompanion because he drinks ice-water at breakfast; and he views my tea with an eye of equal tolerance. It is not till one looks at the second-class passengers that one sees signs of the heterogeneity of the American people; and then one remembers with misgivings the emigrants who crowded on board at Queenstown, with their household goods done up in bundles and gaping, illroped boxes. The thought of them recalls an anecdote which was new to me the other day, and may be fresh to some of my readers. In any case it will bear repetition. An Irishman coming to America for the first time, found New York gay with bunting as he sailed up the harbour. He asked an American fellow-passenger the reason of the display, and was told it was in honour of Evacuation Day. " And what's that ? " he inquired. "Why, the day the British troops evacuated New York." Presently an Englishman came up to the Irishman and asked him if he knew what the flags were for. "For Evacuation Day, to be sure!" was the reply. " What is Evacuation Day ? " asked the Sassenach. "The day we drove you blackguards out of the country, bedded! " was the immediate reply. If not literally true, the story is at least profoundly typical.

There is a light on our starboard bow: my first glimpse, for two and twenty years, of America. It has been literally the dream of my life to revisit the United States. Not once, but fifty times, have I dreamed that the ocean (which loomed absurdly large even in my waking thoughts) was comfortably crossed, and I was landing in New York. I can clearly recall at this moment some of the fantastic shapes the city put on in my dreams—utterly different, of course, from my actual recollections of it. Well, that dream is now realized ; the gates of the Western world are opening to me. What experience awaits me I know not; but this I do know, that the emotion with which I confront it is not one of idle curiosity, or even of calmly sympathetic interest. It is not primarily to my intelligence, but to my imagination, that the word "America" appeals. To many people that word conveys none but prosaic associations; to me it is electric with romance. Only one other word in existence can give me a comparable thrill; the word one sees graven on a roadside pillar as one walks down the southern slope of an Alpine pass: ITALIA. But that word carries the imagination backward only, whereas AMERICA stands for the meeting-place of the past and the future. What the land of Cooper and Mayne Reid was to my boyish fancy, the land of Washington and Lincoln, Hawthorne and Emerson, is to my adult thoughts. Does this mean that I approach America in the temper of a romantic schoolboy? Perhaps; but, bias for bias, I would rather own to that of the romantic schoolboy than to that of the cynical Old-Worldling.

LETTER II

Fog in New York Harbour—The Customs—The Note-Taker's Hyperaesthesia—A Literary Car-Conductor— Mr. Kipling and the American Public—The City of Elevators.

NEW YORK.

BY way of making us feel quite at home, New York receives us with a dank
Scotch mist. On the shores of Staten Island the leafless trees stand out grey and
gaunt against the whity-grey snow, a legacy, no doubt, from the great blizzard.
Though I keep a sharp look-out, I can descry no Liberty Enlightening the World.
Liberty (absit omen !) is wrapped away in grimy cotton-wool. There, however, are
the "sky-scraper" buildings, looming out through the mist, like the Jotuns in Ni-
flheim of Scandinavian mythology. They are grandiose, certainly, and not, to my
thinking, ugly. That word has no application in this context. " Pretty " and "ugly"—
why should we for ever carry about these aesthetic labels in our pockets, and insist
on dabbing them down on everything that comes in our way ? If we cannot get,
with Nietzsche, Jenseits von Gut und Böse, we might at least allow our souls an oc-
casional breathing-space in a region " Back of the Beautiful and the Ugly," as they
say in President's English. While I am trying to formulate my feelings with regard
to this deputation of giants which the giant Republic sends down to the waterside
to welcome us, behold, we have crept up abreast of the Cunard wharf, and there.
stands a little crowd of human welcomers, waving handkerchiefs and American
flags. An energetic tug-boat butts her head gallantly into the flank of the huge liner,
in order to help her round. She glides up to her berth, the gangway is run out, and
at last I set foot upon American—lumber.

What are my emotions ? I have only one; single, simple, easily-expressed: dread
of the United States Custom-House. Its terrors and its tyrannies have been depicted
in such lurid colours on the other side that I am almost surprised to observe no

manifest ogres in uniform caps, but only, it would seem, ordinary human beings. And, on closer acquaintanceship, they prove to be civil and even helpful human beings, with none of the lazy superciliousness which so often characterises the European toll-taker. At first the scene is chaotic enough, but, by aid of an arrangement in alphabetical groups, cosmos soon emerges. The system by which you declare your dutiable goods and are assigned an examiner, and if necessary an appraiser, is admirably simple and free from red-tape. I shall not describe it, for it would be more tedious in description than in act. Enough that the whole thing is conducted, so far as I could see, promptly, efficiently, and with perfect good temper. One brief discussion I heard, between an official and an American citizen, who was heavily assessed on some article or articles which he declared to have been manufactured in America and taken out of the country by himself only a few months before. The official insisted that there was no proof of this; but just as the discussion threatened to become an altercation (a " scrap " they would call it here) some one found a way out. The goods were forwarded in bond to the traveler's place of residence (Hartford, I think), where he declared that he could produce proof of their American origin. For myself, I had to pay two dollars and a half on some magic-lantern slides. I could have imported the lantern, had I owned one, free of charge, as a philosophical instrument used in my profession; but the courts have held, it appears, that though the lantern comes under that rubric, the slides do not. I cannot pretend to grasp the distinction, or to admire the system which necessitates it. But whatever the economic merits or demerits of the tariff, I take pleasure in bearing testimony to the civility with which I found it enforced.

My companion and I express our baggage to our hotel and jump on the platform of a horse-car on West-street, skirting the wharves. The roadway is ill paved, certainly, and the clammy atmosphere has congealed on its surface into an oily black mud; while in the middle of the side streets one can see relics of the blizzard in the shape of little grubby glaciers slowly oozing away. The prospect is not enlivening; nor do the low brick houses, given up to nondescript longshore traffic, and freely punctuated with gilt-lettered saloons, add to its impressiveness. Squalid it is without doubt, this particular aspect of New York ; but what is the squalor of West Street to that of Limehouse or Poplar ? Are our own dock thoroughfares always paved to perfection ? And if we had a blizzard like that of three weeks ago, how long would its vestiges linger in the side-streets of Millwall ? Even as I mark the grimness of the scene, I am conscious of a sort of hyperesthesia against which one ought to be on guard. The note-taking traveler is very apt to forget that the mere act of notetaking upsets his normal perceptivity. He becomes feverishly observant, morbidly critical. He compares incommensurables, and flies to ideal standpoints. He is so eager to descry differences that he overlooks similarities—nay, identities. Thus only can I account for many statements about New York, occurring in the pages of recent and reputable travellers, both French and English, which I find to be exaggerated almost to the point of monstrosity. What should we say of an American who should criticise the Commercial Road from the point of view of Fifth Avenue ? After a week's experience of New York I cannot but fancy that certain travelers I could mention have been guilty of similar errors of proportion.

To return to our street-car platform. The conductor gathers from our conversation that we have just landed from the English steamer, and he at once overflows upon the one great topic of all classes in New York. " I s'pose you've heard," he says, " that Kipling has been very ill ? " Yes, we had heard of his illness before we left England. "He's pulling through now, though," says the conductor with heart-felt satisfaction. That, too, we had ascertained on board. "He ought to be the next poet-laureate,". our friend continues eagerly; " *he* don't follow no beaten tracks. He cuts a road for himself, every time, right through ; and a mighty good road, too! " He then proceeded to make some remarks, which in the rattle of the street I did not quite catch, about " carpet-bag knights." I gathered that he held a low opinion of the present wearer of the bays, and confounded him (not inexcusably) with one or other of his titled compeers. My companion and I were too much taken aback to pursue the theme and ascertain our friend's opinions on Mr. Ruskin, Mr. Meredith, Mrs. Humphry Ward, and Miss Marie Corelli. Think of it! We have travelled three thousand miles to find a tram-conductor whose eyes glisten as he tells us that Kipling is better, and who discusses with a great deal of sense and acuteness the question of the English poet-laureateship! Could anything be more marvelous or more significant? Said I not well when I declared the Atlantic Ocean of less account than the Straits of Dover ?

This was indeed a welcome to the New World. Fate could not have devised a more ingenious and at the same time tactful way of making us feel at home ; though at home, indeed, a Mile End 'bus conductor is scarcely the authority one would turn to for enlightened views upon the Laureateship. The mere fact of our friend's having heard of Mr. Kipling's existence struck us as surprising enough, until we learned that the poet of Tommy Atkins is at the present moment quite the most famous person in the United States. When his illness was at its height, hourly bulletins were posted in factories and workshops, and people meeting in the streets asked each other, " How is he ? " without deeming. it necessary to supply an antecedent to the pronoun. It was grammatically as well as spiritually a case of " Kipling understood."

At a low music-hall into which I strayed one evening, one of the nigger cornermen sang a song of which the nature may be sufficiently divined from the refrain, " And the tom-cat was the cause of it all." This lyric being loudly encored, the performer came forward, and, to my astonishment, began to recite a long series of doggerel verses upon Mr. Kipling's illness, setting forth how.

" His strong will made him famous, and his strong will pulled him through."

They were imbecile, they were maudlin, they were in the worst possible taste. So far as the reciter was concerned, they were absolutely insincere clap-trap. But the crowded audience received them with rapture ; and the very fact that an astute caterer should serve up this particular form of clap-trap showed how the sympathy with Mr. Kipling had permeated even the most un-literary stratum of the public. To an Englishman, nothing can be more touching than to find on every hand this enthusiastic affection for the poet of the Seven Seas—a writer, too, who has not dealt over-tenderly with American susceptibilities, and has, by sheer force of genius, lived down a good deal of unpopularity.

For the moment, neither President McKinley nor Mr. Fitzsimmons can vie with him in notoriety. His sole rival as a popular hero is Admiral Dewey, whose name is in every mouth and on every hoarding. He is the one living celebrity whom the Italian image-vendors admit to their pantheon, where he rubs shoulders with Shakespeare, Dante, Beethoven, and the Venus of Milo. It is related that, at a Camp of Exercise last year, President McKinley chanced to stray beyond bounds, and on returning was confronted by a sentry, who dropped his rifle and bade him halt. " I have forgotten the pass-word," said Mr. McKinley, " but if you will look at me you will see that I am the President." " If you were George Dewey himself," was the reply, " you shouldn't get by here without the password." This anecdote has a flavor of ancient history, but it is aptly brought up to date.[2]

> [2] A similar story is told of the Confederate President. Challenged by a sentinel, he said, " Look at me and you will see that I am President Davis."
> " Well," said the soldier, " you *do* look like a used postage-stamp. Pass, President Davis!"

We bid adieu to our poetical conductor, take a cross-town car, and are presently pushing at the revolving doors—a draught-excluding plate-glass turnstile—of a vast red-brick hotel, luxurious and labyrinthine. A short colloquy with a clerk at the bureau, and we find ourselves in a gorgeously upholstered elevator, whizzing aloft to the thirteenth floor. Not the top floor—far from it. If you could slice off the stories above the thirteenth, as you slice off the top of an *egg,* and plant them down in Europe, they would of themselves make a biggish hotel according to our standards. This first elevator voyage is the prelude to how many others! For the past week I seem to have spent the best part of my time in elevators. I must have travelled miles on miles at right angles to the earth's surface. If all my ascensions could be put together, they would out-top Olympus and make Ossa a wart.

This is the first sensation of life in New York— you feel that the Americans have practically added a new dimension to space. They move almost as much on the perpendicular as on the horizontal plane. When they find themselves a little crowded, they simply tilt a street on end and call it a sky-scraper. This hotel, for example (the Waldorf-Astoria), is nothing but a couple of populous streets soaring up into the air instead of crawling along the ground. When I was here in 1877, I remember looking with wonder at the ***Tribune building,*** hard by the Post Office, which was then considered a marvel of architectural daring. Now it is dwarfed into absolute insignificance by a dozen Cyclopean structures on every hand. It looks as diminutive as the Adelphi Terrace in contrast with the Hotel Cecil. I am credibly informed that in some of the huge down-town buildings they run " express " elevators, which do not stop before the fifteenth, eighteenth, twentieth floor, as the case may be. Some such arrangement seems very necessary, for the elevator ***Bummel-sugs,*** which stops at every floor, take quite an appreciable slice out of the average New York day. I wonder that American ingenuity has not provided a system of pneumatic passenger-tubes for lightning communication with these aerial suburbs, these " mansions in the sky."

LETTER III

New York a much-maligned City—Its Charm—Mr. Steevens's Antitheses—New York compared with Other Cities—Its Slums—Advertisements—Architecture in New York and Philadelphia.

NEW YORK.

MANY superlatives have been applied to New York by her own children, by the stranger within her gates, and by the stranger without her gates, at a safe distance. I, a newcomer, venture to apply what I believe to be a new superlative, and to call her the most maligned city in the world. Even sympathetic observers have exaggerated all that is uncouth, unbeautiful, unhealthy in her life, and overlooked, as it seems to me, her all-pervading charm. One must be a pessimist indeed to feel no exhilaration on coming in contact with such intensity of upward striving life as meets one on every hand in this league-long island city, stretching oceanward between her eastern Sound and her western estuary, and roofed by a radiant dome of smokeless sky. "Upward-striving life," I say, for everywhere and in every branch of artistic effort the desire for beauty is apparent, while at many points the achievement is remarkable and inspiriting. I speak, of course, mainly of material beauty;

but it is hard to believe that so marked an impulse toward the good as one notes in architecture, painting, sculpture, and literature, can be unaccompanied by a cognate impulse toward moral beauty, even in relation to civic life. The New Yorker's pride in New York is much more alert and active than the Londoner's pride in London; and this feeling must ere long make itself effective and dominant. For the great advantage, it seems to me, that America possesses over the Old World is its material and moral plasticity. Even among the giant structures of this city, one feels that there is nothing rigid, nothing oppressive, nothing inaccessible to the influence of changing conditions. If the buildings are Cyclopean, so is the race that reared them. The material world seems as clay on the potter's wheel, visibly taking on the impress of the human spirit; and the human spirit, as embodied in this superbly vital people, seems to be visibly thrilling to all the forces of civilisation.

One of the latest, and certainly one of the most keen-sighted, of English travellers in America is Mr. G. W. Steevens, a master journalist if ever there was one. I turn to his ***Land of the Dollar*** and I find New York writ down "uncouth, formless, piebald, chaotic." " Never have I seen," says Mr. Steevens, " a city more hideous. Nothing is given to beauty; everything centers in hard utility." Mr. Steevens must forgive me for saying that this is simply libellous. It is true, I do not quote him fairly; I omit his laudatory antitheses. The truncated phrase in the above passage reads in the original "more hideous or more splendid," and after averring that " nothing is given to beauty," Mr. Steevens immediately proceeds to celebrate the beauty of many New York buildings. Are we to understand, then, that the architects thought of nothing but " hard utility," and that it was some aesthetic divinity that shaped their blocks, rough-hew them how they might ? For my part, I cannot see how truth is to result from the clash of contradictory falsehoods. There are a few cities more splendid than New York; many more hideous. In point of concentrated architectural magnificence, there is nothing in New York to compare with the Vienna Ringstrasse, from the Opera House to the Votive Church. In the splendour which proceeds from ordered uniformity and spaciousness, Paris is, of course, incomparable; while a Scotchman may perhaps be excused for holding that, as regards splendour of situation, Edinburgh is hard to beat. Nor is there any single prospect in New York so impressive as the panorama of London from Waterloo

Bridge, when it happens to be visible— that imperial. sweep of river frontage from the Houses of Parliament to the Tower. Except in the new region, far up the Hudson, New York shares with Dublin the disadvantage of turning her meaner aspects to her river fronts, though the majesty of the rivers themselves, and the grandiose outlines of the Brooklyn Bridge, largely compensate for this defect. In the main, then, the splendour of New York is as yet sporadic. It is emerging on every hand from comparative meanness and commonplace. At no point can one as yet say, " This prospect is finer than anything Europe can show." But everywhere there are purple patches of architectural splendour; and one can easily foresee the time when Fifth Avenue, the whole circuit of Central Park, and the up-town riverside region will be magnificent beyond compare.

As for the superlative hideousness attributed by Mr. Steevens to New York, I can only inquire, in the local idiom : " What is the matter with Glasgow ? " Or, indeed, with Hull ? or Newcastle ? or the north-east regions of London ? No doubt New York contains some of the very worst slums in the world. That melancholy distinction must be conceded her. But simply to the outward eye the slums of New York have not the monotonous hideousness of our English "warrens of the poor." In spite of her hard winter, New York cannot quite forget that her latitude is that of Madrid and Naples, not of London, or even of Paris. Her slums have a Southern air about them, a variety of contour and colour—in some aspects one might almost say a gaiety—unknown to Whitechapel or Bethnal Green. For one thing, the ubiquitous balconies and fire escapes serve of themselves to break the monotony of line, and lend, as it were, a peculiar texture to the scene; to say nothing of the opportunities they afford for the display of multifarious shreds and patches of colour. Then the houses themselves are often brightly, not to say loudly, painted; so that in the clear, sparkling atmosphere characteristic of New York, the most squalid slum puts on a many-coloured Southern aspect, which suggests Naples or Marseilles rather than the back streets of any English city. Add to this that the inhabitants are largely of southern origin, and are apt, whenever the temperature will permit, to carry on the main part of their daily lives out of doors; and you can understand that, appalling as poverty may be in New York, the average slum is not so dank, dismal, and suicidally monotonous as a street of a similar status in London.

"The whole city," says Mr. Steevens, "is plastered, and papered, and painted with advertisements"; and he instances the huge " H-O " (whatever that may mean) which confronts one as one sails up the harbour, and the omnipresent " Castoria " placards. Here Mr. Steevens shows symptoms of the note-taker's hyperaesthesia. The facts he states are undeniable, but the implication that advertisement is carried to greater excess in New York than in London and other European cities seems to me utterly groundless. The "H-O" advertisement is not one whit more monstrous than, for instance, the huge announcements of cheap clothing-shops, painted all over the ends of houses, that deface the railway approaches to Paris; nor is it so flagrant and aggressive as the illuminated advertisements of whisky and California wines that vulgarise the august spectacle of the Thames by night. It is true that the proprietors of " Castoria" have occupied nearly every blank wall that is visible from Brooklyn Bridge; but their advertisements are so far from garish that I should scarcely have noticed them had not Mr. Steevens called my attention to them. Sky-signs, as Mr. Steevens admits, are unknown in New York ; so are the flashing out-and-in electric advertisements which make night hideous in London. One or two large steady-burning advertisements irradiate Madison Square of an evening; but being steady they are comparatively inoffensive. Twenty years ago, when I crossed the continent from San Francisco, I noticed with disgust the advertisements stencilled on every second rock in the canyons of Nevada, and defacing every coign of vantage around Niagara. Whether this abuse continues I know not; but I know that the pill placards and sauce puffs which blossom in our English meadows along every main line of railway are quite as offensive. Far be it from me to deny that advertising is carried to deplorable excesses in America; but in picking this out as a differentia, Mr. Steevens shows that his intentness of observation in New York has for the moment dimmed his mental vision of London. It is a case, I fancy, in which the expectation was father to the thought.

Similarly, Mr. Steevens notes, " No chiropodist worthy of the name but keeps at his door a modelled human foot the size of a cab-horse; and other trades go and do likewise." The " cab-horse " is a monumental exaggeration; but it is true that some chiropodists use as a sign a foot of colossal proportions—the size of a small sheep, let us say, if we must adopt a zoological standard. So far good ; but the implication that the streets of New York swarm, like a scene in a harlequinade, with similarly Brobdingnagian signs is quite unfounded. Thus it is, I think, that travellers are apt to seize on isolated eccentricities or extravagances (have we no monstrous signs in England ?) and treat them as typical. Mr. Steevens came to America prepared to find everything gigantic, and the chiropodist's foot so agreeably fulfilled his expectation that he thought it unnecessary to look any further— "ex pede Herculem."[3]

The architecture of New York, according to Mr. Steevens, is "the outward expression of the freest, fiercest individualism.Seeing it, you can well understand the admiration of an American

[3] One method of advertisement which I observed in Chicago has not yet, so far as I know, been introduced into England. One of the windows of a vast dry-goods store on State Street was fitted up as a dentist's parlour; and when I passed a young lady was reclining in the operating-chair and having her teeth stopped, to the no small delectation of a little crowd which blocked the side-walk.

for something ordered and proportioned—for the Rue de Rivoli or Regent Street" I heard this admiration emphatically expressed the other day by one of the foremost and most justly famous of American authors ; but, unlike Mr. Steevens, I could not understand it. "What!" I said, "you would Haussmannize New York! You would reduce the glorious variety of Fifth Avenue to the deadly uniformity of the Avenue de l'Opra, where each block of buildings reproduces its neighbor, as though they had all been stamped by one gigantic die !" Such an architectural ideal is inconceivable to me. It is all very well for a few short streets, for a square or two, for a quadrant like that of Regent Street, or a crescent or circus like those of Bath or Edinburgh. But to apply it throughout a whole quarter of a city, or even throughout the endless vistas of a great American street, would be simply maddening. Better the most heaven-storming or sky-scraping audacity of individualism than any attempt to transform New York into a Fourierist phalanstery or a model prison. I do not doubt that there will one day be some legal restriction on Towers of Babel, and that the hygienic disadvantages of the microbe-breeding "well" or air-shaft will be more fully recognised than they are at present A time may come, too, when the ideal of an unforced harmony in architectural groupings may replace the now dominant instinct of aggressive diversity. But whatever developments the future may have in store, I must own my gratitude to the " fierce individualism" of the present for a new realisation of the possibilities of architectural beauty in modern life. At almost every turn in New York one comes across some building that gives one a little shock of pleasure. Sometimes, indeed, it is the pleasure of recognising an old friend in a new place—a patch of Venice or a chunk of Florence transported bodily to the New World. The exquisite tower of the Madison Square Garden, for instance, is modelled on that of the Giralda, at Seville; while the New University Club, on Fifth Avenue, is simply a Florentine fortress-palace of somewhat disproportionate height. But along with a good deal of sheer reproduction of European models, one finds a great deal of ingenious and inventive adaptation, to say nothing of a very delicate taste in the treatment of detail. New York abounds, it is true, with monuments of more than one bygone and detestable period of architectural fashion; but they are as distinctly survivals from a dead past as is the wooden shanty which occupies one of the best sites on Fifth Avenue, in the very shadow of the new Delmonico's. I wish tasteless, conventional, and machine-made architecture were as much of a "back number" in England as it is here. A practised observer could confidently date any prominent building in New York, to within a year or two, by its architectural merit; and the greater the merit the later the year.

In short, architecture is here a living art. Go where you will in these up-town regions, you can see imagination and cultured intelligence in the act, as it were, of impressing beauty of proportion and detail upon brick and terra-cotta, granite and marble. And domestic or middleclass architecture is not neglected. The American " master builders " do not confine themselves to towers and palaces, but give infinite thought and loving care to "homes for human beings." The average old-fashioned New York house, so far as I have seen it, is externally unattractive (the characteristic material, a sort of coffee-coloured stone, being truly hideous), and internally dark, cramped, and stuffy. But modern houses, even of no special pretensions, are generally delightful, with their polished wood floors and fittings, and their airy suites of rooms. The American architect has a great advantage over his English colleague in the fact that in furnace-heated houses only the bedrooms require to be shut off with doors. The halls and public rooms can be grouped so that, when the curtains hung in their wide doorways are drawn back, two, three, or four rooms are open to the eye at once, and charming effects of space and light-and-shade can be obtained. Of this advantage the modern house-planner makes excellent use, and I have seen more than one quite modest family house which, without any sacrifice of comfort, gives one a sense of almost palatial spaciousness. An architectural exhibition which I saw the other day proved that equal or even greater care and attention is being bestowed upon the country house, in which a characteristically American style is being developed, mainly founded, I take it, upon the suave and graceful classicism of Colonial architecture. The wide " piazza " is its most noteworthy feature, and the opportunity it offers for beautiful cloister-work is being utilised to the full. Furthermore, the large attendance at the exhibition showed what a keen interest the public takes in the art—a symptom of high vitality.

In Philadelphia, too, where I spent some time last week, there is a good deal of exquisite architecture to be seen. The old Philadelphia dwelling house, " simplex munditiis," with its plain red-brick front and white marble steps, has a peculiar charm for me; but it, of course, is not a product of the present movement. I do not know the date of some lovely white marble palazzetti scattered about the Rittenhouse Square region; but the Art Club on Broad Street, and the Houston Club for Students of the University of Pennsylvania, are both quite recent buildings, and both very beautiful. I could mention several other buildings that are, as they say here, " pretty good" (a phrase of high commendation) ; but I had better get safely out of New York before I enlarge on the merits of Philadelphia. There is only one city the New Yorker despises more than Philadelphia, and that is Brooklyn. The New York schoolboy speaks of Philadelphia as " the place the chestnuts go to when they die"; and to the most popular wit in New York at this moment (an Americanised Englishman, by the way) is attributed the saying, " Mr. So-and-so has three daughters— two alive, and one in Philadelphia." Six different people have related this gibe to me; it is only less admired than the same gentleman's observation as he alighted from an electric car at the further end of the Suspension Bridge, when he heaved a deep sigh, and remarked, "In the midst of life we are in Brooklyn." Another favorites anecdote in New York is that of the Philadelphian who went to a doctor and complained of insomnia. The doctor gave him a great deal of sage advice as to diet, exercise, and so forth, concluding, " If after that you haven't better nights, let me see you again." " But you mistake, doctor," the patient replied; " I sleep all right at night—it's in the daytime I can't sleep!"

LETTER IV

Absence of Red Tape—" Rapid Transit" in New York —The Problem and its Solution—The Whirl of Life-New York by Night—The "White Magic" of the Future.

NEW YORK.

WHATEVER turn her fiscal policy may take in the future, I hope America will keep an absolutely prohibitive duty upon the import of red tape, while at the same time discouraging the home manufacture of the article. The absence of red tape is, to me, one of the charms of life in this country. One gathers, indeed, that the art of running a Circumlocution Office is carried to a high pitch in the political sphere. But there it is exercised with a definite object; it is a means to an end, cunningly devised and skilfully applied; it is not a mere matter of instinct, inertia, and routine. The Tite Barnacles of Dickens's satire were perfectly honest people according to their lights. They were sincerely convinced that the British Empire would crumble to pieces the moment its ligaments of red tape were in the slightest degree relaxed. Their strength lay in the fact that they represented an innate tendency in the nation, or at any rate in the dominant class at the period of which Dickens wrote. In America there is no such innate tendency. The Tite Barnacles do not imagine or pretend that they are saving the Republic; they simply make use of a convenient political machinery to serve their private ends. Therefore their position, however strong it may seem for the moment, is insecurely founded. It rests upon no moral basis, it finds no stronghold in the national character. Outsiders may think the average American citizen strangely tolerant of abuses, and indeed I find him smiling with placid amusement at things which, were I in his place, would make my blood boil. But he is under no illusion as to the real nature of these things. An abuse remains an abuse in his eyes, though he may not for the moment see his way to rectifying it. The red tape which is used to embarrass justice or " tie up " reform commands no reverence even from the party that employs it. Cynicism may endure for the night, but indignation ariseth in the morning.

The American character, in a word, does not naturally run to red tape. Observe, for instance, the system of transit in New York: it is admirably successful in grappling with a very difficult problem, and its success proceeds from the absence of by-laws and restrictions, the omnipresence of good-nature and common-sense. The problem is rendered difficult, not only by the enormous numbers to be conveyed, but by the stocking-like configuration of Manhattan Island. The business quarter of New York is in the foot, the residential quarters in the calf and knee. Therefore there is a great rush of people down to the foot in the morning and up to the knee in the afternoon. The business quarter of London is like the hub of a wheel, from which the railway and omnibus lines radiate like spokes. In New York there is very little radiation or dispersion of the multitude. Practically the Whole tide sets down a narrow channel in the morning, and up again in the evening. At the time, then, of these tidal waves, it is a flat impossibility that transit can be altogether comfortable. The " elevated " trains and electric trolleys are overcrowded, certainly; but you can always find a place in them, and they carry you so rapidly that the discomfort is rendered as little irksome as possible. A society has been formed, I see, to agitate against this overcrowding; but it seems to me it will only waste its pains. Let it agitate for an underground railway, by all means; and if, as I gather, the underground railway scheme is obstructed by self-seeking vested interests, let it do its best to break down the obstruction. Until some altogether new means of transport are provided, the attempt to restrict the number of passengers which a car or trolley may carry is, I think, anti-social, and must prove futile. The force of public convenience would break the red-tape barrier like a cobweb. The trains and trolleys follow each other at the very briefest intervals; it does not seem possible that a greater number should be run on the existing lines; and, that being so, there is no alternative between overcrowding and the far greater inconvenience of indefinite delay. Fancy having to " take a number," as they do in Paris, and await your turn for a seat! New York would be simply paralysed. It is needless to point out, of course, that where steam or electricity is the motive power there is no cruelty to animals in overcrowding.

The American people, rightly and admirably as it seems to me, choose the lesser of two evils, and minimise it by good temper and mutual civility. At a certain hour of every morning, the " L" railroad trains are as densely packed as our Metropolitan trains on Boat-Race Day. There are people clinging in clusters to each of the straps, and even the platforms between the cars are crowded to the very couplings. It often appears hopelessly impossible for any new-comer to squeeze in, or for those who are wedged in the middle of a long car to force their way out. Yet when the necessity arises, no force has to be applied. People manage somehow or other to "welcome the coming, speed the parting guest." Every one recognises that cantankerous obstructiveness would only make matters worse, nay, absolutely intolerable. The first comer makes no attempt to insist upon his position of advantage, because he knows that tomorrow he may be the last comer. The sense of individual inconvenience is swamped in the sense of general convenience. People laugh and rather enjoy the joke when a too sudden start or an abrupt curve sends a whole group of them cannoning up against one another. It must be remembered that the transit is rapid, so that there is no irritating sense of wasted time: and that the cars are brilliantly lighted, and, on the whole, well ventilated, so that there is no fog, smoke, or sulphurous air to get on the nerves and strain the temper. The scene as a whole, even on a wet, disagreeable evening, is not depressing, but rather cheerful. For my part, I regard it with positive pleasure, as a manifestation of the national character. Less admirable, to be sure, is the public acquiescence in the political manoeuvring which blocks the proposed underground railway. Yet the opponents of the scheme have doubtless something to say on their side. It appears, at any rate, that the profits of the "L" road are not exorbitant. It is said to be only through overcrowding that it pays at all. The passengers it seats barely suffice to cover expenses, and "the profits hang on to the straps."

Idealists hope that when the underground comes the elevated will go; but I, as an outsider, cannot share this hope. In the first place, I don't see how the mere substitution of one line for another is to relieve the congestion of traffic ; in the second place, the elevated seems to me an admirable institution, which it would be a great pity to abolish. Even aesthetically there is much to be said for it. The road itself, to be sure, does not add to the beauty of the avenues along which it runs, but it is not by any means the eyesore one might imagine; and the trains, with their light, graceful, and elegantly proportioned cars, so different from our squat and formless railway carriages, seem to me a positively beautiful feature of the city life. They are not very noisy, they are not very smoky, and they will be smokeless and almost noiseless when they are run by electricity. The discomfort they cause to dwellers on the avenues is, I am sure, greatly exaggerated. People who do not live on the avenues suffer in their sympathetic imagination much more than the actual martyrs to the "L" road suffer in fact. Imagination makes cowards of us all. For my part, I endured agonies from the rush, whirl and clatter of New York before I left London; but here I find nothing that, to healthy nerves, is not rather enjoyable than otherwise. Neither up town nor down town is the traffic so dense, the roar and bustle so continuous, as that of London; while the service of trains and cars is so excellent and so simply arranged that it costs much less thought, effort, and worry to " get about" in Manhattan than in Middlesex. In saying this I may perhaps offend American susceptibilities. There is nothing we moderns are more apt to brag .of than the nervous overstrain of our life. But sincerity comes before courtesy, and I must gently but firmly decline to allow New York a monopoly of neurasthenia, or of the conditions that produce it.

One great difference is, I take it, that while New York exhausts it also stimulates, whereas the days of the year when there is any positive stimulus in the air of London may be counted on the ten fingers. Muggy and misty days do occur here, it is true ; but though the natives tell me that this month of March has been exceptionally unpleasant, the prevailing impression I have received is that of a lofty and radiant vault of sky, with keen, sweet, limpid air that one drank in eagerly, like sparkling wine. More than once, after a slight snowfall, I have seen the air full of dancing particles of light, like the gold leaf in Dantzic brandy. One of the most impressive things I ever saw, though I did not then realise its tragic significance, was the huge column of smoke that rose into the clear blue air from the Windsor Hotel fire. I happened to come out on Fifth Avenue, close to the Manhattan Club, just as the tail of the St. Patrick's Day procession was passing; and, looking up the avenue after it, I was aware of a gigantic white pillar standing motionless, as it seemed to me, and cleaving the limitless blue dome almost to the zenith. The procession moved quietly on; no one appeared to take any notice; and as fires are ineffective in the daylight, I turned down the avenue instead of up, and saw no more of the spectacle. But I shall never forget that " pillar of cloud by day," standing out in the sunshine, white as marble or sea foam.

At night, again, under the purple, star-lit sky, street life in the central region of New York is indescribably exhilarating. From Union Square to Herald Square, and even further up, Broadway and many of the cross streets flash out at dusk into the most brilliant illumination. Theatres, restaurants, stores, are outlined in incandescent lamps ; the huge electric trolleys come sailing along in an endless stream, profusely jewelled with electricity; and down the thickly gemmed vista of every cross street one can see the elevated trains, like luminous winged serpents, skimming through the air.[4] The great restaurants are crowded with gaily dressed merrymakers ; and altogether there is a sense of festivity in the air, without any flagrantly meretricious element in it, which I plead guilty to finding very enjoyable. From the moral, and even from the loftily aesthetic point of view, this gaudy, glittering Vanity Fair is no doubt open to criticism. What reconciles me to it aesthetically is the gemlike transparency of its colouring. Garish it is, no doubt, but not in the least stifling, smoky, or lurid. The application of electricity—light divorced from smoke and heat—to

[4] I find the same idea (a sufficiently obvious one) finely expressed by Mr. Richard Hovey in his book of poems entitled ***Along the Trail:***

Look, how the overhead train at the Morningside curveLoops

like a sea-born dragon its sinuous flight,

Loops in the night in and out, high up in the air,

Like a serpent of stars with the coil and undulant reach of waves.

the beautifying of city life is as yet in its infancy. Even the Americans have scarcely got beyond the point of making lavish use of the raw material. But the raw material is beautiful in itself, and in this pellucid air (the point to which one always returns) it produces magical effects.

The other night, at a restaurant, I sat at the next table to Mr. Edison, and could not but look with interest and admiration at his furrowed, anxious, typically American and truly beautiful face. Here, if you like, was an example of nervous overstrain; but the soft and yet brilliant light of the restaurant was in itself a sufficient reminder that the overstrain had not been incurred for nothing. Electricity is the true " white magic " of the future; and here, with his pallid face and silver hair, sat the master magician—one of the great light-givers of the world. A light-giver, I think, in more than a merely material sense. The moral influence of the electric lamp, its effect upon the hygiene of the soul, has not yet been duly estimated. But even in a merely material sense, what has not the Edison movement, as it may be called, done for this city of New York! Its influence is felt on every hand, in comfort, convenience, and beauty. The lavish use of electricity, both as an illuminant and as a motive power, combines with its climate, its situation, and its architecture to make New York one of the most fascinating cities in the world. Why good Americans, when they die, should go to Paris, is a theological enigma which more and more puzzles me.

POSTSCRIPT.—Since my return to England, I have carefully reconsidered my impression that the rush, whirl, and clamour of street life is greater in London than in New York. Every day confirms it. On our main thoroughfares, the stream of omnibuses is quite as unbroken as the stream of electric and cable cars in New York; our van traffic is at least as heavy; and we have in addition the host of creeping " growlers " and darting hansoms which is almost without counterpart in New York. I know of no crossing in New York so trying to the nerves as Piccadilly Circus or Charing Cross (Trafalgar Square). The intersection of Broadway, Fifth Avenue and 23rd Street, at Madison Square, is the nearest approach to these bewildering ganglia of traffic. It must be owned, too, that the Bowery, with its two "elevated" tracks and four lines of trolleycars, is a place where one cannot safely let one's wits go wool-gathering, especially on a rainy evening when the roadway is under repair. Let me add that there is one place in New York where the whirl of traffic (" whirl" in a literal sense) is unique and amazing. I mean the covered area at the New York end of Brooklyn Bridge where the transpontine electric cars, in an incessant stream, swoop down the curves of the bridge and sweep round on their return journey. The scene at night is indescribable. The air seems supersaturated with electricity, flashing and crackling on every hand. One has a sense of having strayed unwittingly into the midst of a miniature planetary system in full swing, with the boom of the trolleys, in their mazy courses, to represent the music of the spheres.

LETTER V

Character and Culture—American Universities—Is the American " Electric " or Phlegmatic ?—Alleged Laxity of the Family Tie—Postscript: The University System.

NEW YORK.

IT is four weeks to-day since I landed in New York, and, save for forty hours in Philadelphia and four hours in Brooklyn, I have spent all that time in Manhattan Island. Yet, to my shame be it spoken, I am not prepared with any generalisation as to the American character. It has been my good fortune to see a great deal of literary and artistic New York, and, comparing it with literary and artistic London, I am inclined to say "Pompey and Caesar berry much alike—specially Pompey ! " The New Yorker is far more cosmopolitan than the Londoner; of that ! there is no doubt. He knows all that we know about current English literature. He knows all that we do *not* know about current American literature. He is much more interested in and influenced by French literature and art than the average educated Englishman—so much so that the leading French critics, such as M. Brunetiere and M. Rod, lecture here to crowded and appreciative audiences. Moreover, an excellent German theatre permanently established in the city keeps the literary world well abreast of the dramatic movement in Germany. But the cosmopolitanism of the educated New

Yorker merely means that he has everything in common with the educated Londoner—and a little over. His traditions are ours, his standards are ours, his ideals are ours. He is busied with the same problems of ethics, of aesthetics, of style, even of grammar. I had not been three days in New York when I found myself plunged in a hot discussion of the " split infinitive," in which I was ranged with two Americans against a recreant Briton who defended the collocation. "It is a mistake to regard it is an Americanism," said one of the Americans. " It is as old as the English language, or at least as old as Wickliff. But it is unnecessary, and the best modern practice discountenances it." I felt like falling on the neck of an ally of half an hour's standing, and swearing eternal friendship. What matters Alaska, or Venezuela, or Nicaragua, " or all the stones of stumbling in the world," so long as we have a common interest in (and some of us a common distaste for) the split infinitive ?

To put the matter briefly, while the outlook of the New Yorker is wider than ours, his standpoint is the same. We gather from a well-known anecdote that some, at least, of the cultivated Americans of Thackeray's time were inclined to "think o Tupper." To-day they do not " think of Tupper " any more than we do—and by Tupper I mean, of course, not the veritable Martin Farquhar, but the Tuppers of the passing hour. In America as in England, no doubt, there is a huge half-educated public, ravenous for doughnuts of romance served up with syrup of sentiment. The enthusiasms of the American shop girl, I take it, are very much the same as those of her English sister. But the line of demarcation between the educated and the half-educated is just as clear in New York as in London. For the cultivated American of to-day, the Boomster booms and the Sibyl sibyllates in vain. I find no justification, in this city at any rate, for the old saying which described America as the most common-schooled and least educated country in the world. If we must draw distinctions, I should say that the effect of the American system of university education was to raise the level of general culture, while lowering the standard of special scholarship. II believe that the general American tendency is to insist less than we do on sheer mental discipline for its own sake, whether in classics or mathematics, to allow the student a wider latitude of choice, and to] enable him to specialise at an earlier point in his! curriculum upon the studies he most affects, or which are most likely to be directly useful to him in practical life. Thus the American universities, probably, do not turn out many men who can "read Plato with their feet on the hob," but many who can, and do, read and understand him as Colonel New-come read Caesar—"with a translation, sir, with a translation." The width of out-look which I have noted as characteristic of literary New York is deliberately aimed at in the university system, and most successfully attained. The average young man of parts turned out by an American university has a many-sided interest in, and comprehension of, European literature and the intellectual movement of the world, which may go far to compensate for his possible or even probable inexpertness in Greek aorists and Latin elegiacs.

The academic and literary New Yorker, I am well aware, is not " the Ameri-can." But who is " the American " ? I turn to Mr. G. W. Steevens, and find that "the American is a highly electric Anglo-Saxon. His temperament is of quicksilver. There is as much difference in vivacity and emotion between him and an Englishman as there is between an Englishman and an Italian." Well, Mr. Steevens is a keener ob-server than I; when he wrote .this he had been two months in America to my one ; and he had travelled far and wide over the continent. I am not rash enough, then, to contradict him ; but I must own that I have not met this " American," or any-thing like him, in the streets, clubs, theatres, restau-rants, or public conveyances of New York. On the contrary, as I take my walks abroad between Union Square and Central Park, or hang on to the straps of an elevated train or cable car, I am all the time occupied in trying—and failing—to find marked differences of appearance and manners between the people I see here and the people I should expect to see under similar circumstances in London. Differences of dress and feature there are, of course—but how trifling! Difference of manners there is none, unless it lie in the general good-nature and unobtrusive politeness of the American crowd, upon which I have already remarked. We all know that there is a distinctively American physical type, recognisable especially in the sex which aims at self-development, instead of self-suppression, in its attire. When one meets her in Bloomsbury (where she abounds in the tourist season) one readily distinguishes the American lady; but here specific distinctions are absorbed in generic identity, and the only difference between American and English ladies of which I am habitually conscious lies in the added touch of Parisian elegance which one notes in the costumes on Fifth Avenue.

The average of beauty is certainly very high in New York. I will not say higher than in London, for there too it is remarkable; but this I will say, that night after night I have looked round the audiences in New York theatres, and found a clear majority of notably good-looking women. There are few European cities where one could hope to make the same observation. It is especially to be noted, I think, that the American lady has the art of growing old with comely dignity. She loses her complexion, indeed, but only to put on a new beauty in the contrast between her olive skin and her silvering or silver hair. This contrast may almost be called the characteristic feature of the specially American type, which is much more clearly discernible in middle-aged and old than in young women.

As for the men, what strikes one in New York is the total absence of the traditional " Yankee " type. It must have a foundation in fact, since the Americans themselves have accepted it in political caricature. No doubt I shall find it in its original habitat—New England. It has certainly not penetrated into New York. On close examination, the average man-in-the-street is distinguishable from his fellow in London by certain trifling differences in " the cut of his jib "—his fashion in hats, in moustaches, in neckties. But the intense electricity that Mr. Steevens discovers in him has totally eluded my observation. The fault may be mine, but assuredly I have failed to " faire jaillir l'eincelle." I have looked in vain for any symptom of the " temperament of quicksilver." Mr. Steevens, it is true, made his observations during the last Presidential election. Perhaps the quick-silver is generated in the American citizen by political excitement, and when that is over " runs out at the heels of his boots."

But, surely, it is a monstrous exaggeration to state in general terms that the difference in "vivacity and emotion" between the average American and the average Englishman is as great as the difference between an Englishman and an Italian. By what inconceivable error does it happen, then, that the American of fiction and drama—English, Continental, and American to boot—is always represented as outdoing John Bull himself in Anglo - Saxon phlegm ? In the courts of ethnology, I shall be told, " what the caricaturist says is not evidence "; but no caricature could ever have gained such world-wide acceptance without a substratum of truth to support it. The probabilities of the case are greatly against the development of any special " vivacity " of temperament, for though there has no doubt been a large Keltic admixture in the Anglo-Saxon stock, there has been a large Teutonic infusion (German and Scandinavian) to counterbalance it. Simply as a matter of observation, the differences between English and Italian manners hit you in the eye, while the differences between American and English manners are really microscopic; and manners, I take it, are the outward and visible signs of temperament. A Scotchman by birth, a Londoner by habit, I walk the streets of New York undetected, to the best of my belief, until I began to speak; in Rome, on the contrary, every one recognises me at a glance as an " Inglese," unless they mistake me for an " Ameri-cano." To me it is amazing how inessential is the change produced by the Anglo-Saxon type and temperament by influences of climate and admixture of foreign blood. There are great foreign cities in New York—German, Italian, Yiddish, Bohemian, Hungarian, Chinese—but the New York of the New Yorker is scarcely, to the Eng-lishman, a foreign city.

The other day I heard an Englishman, who has lived for twenty-five years in America, maintaining very emphatically that the chief difference between England and America lay in the greater laxity of the family bond on this side of the Atlan-tic. He declared that, in the main, " home" meant less to the American than to the Englishman, and especially that the American boy between thirteen and twenty was habitually insurgent against home influences. It would be ludicrous, of course, to set up the observations of a month against the experience of a quarter of a century; yet I cannot but feel that either I have been. miraculously fortunate in the glimpses I have obtained of American home life, or else there is something amiss with my friend's generalisation. Perhaps he brought away with him from England in the early seventies a conception of the " patria potestas " which he would now find out of date there as well as here. No doubt the migratory habit is stronger in America than in England, and family life is not apt to flourish in hotels or boarding-houses. The Saratoga trunk is not the best cornerstone for the home : so much we may take for granted. But the American families who are content to go through life without a threshold and hearthstone of their own must, after all, be in a vanish-ing minority. They very naturally cut a larger figure in fiction than in fact. It has been my privilege to see something of the daily life of a good many families living under their own roof-tree, and in every case without exception I have been struck with the beauty and intimacy of the relation between parents and children. When my friend laid down his theory of the intractable American boy, I could not but think of a youth of twenty whom I had seen only two days before, whose manner towards his father struck me as an ideal blending of affectionate comradeship with old-fashioned respect.[5] True, this was in Philadelphia, " the City of Homes," and even there it may have been an exceptional case. I am not so illogical as to pit a single observation against (presumably) a wide induction; I merely offer for what it is worth one item of evidence.

Again, it has been my good fortune here in New York to spend an evening in a household which suggested a chapter of Dickens in his tenderest and most idyllic mood. It was the home of an actor and

[5] "Affectionate comradeship" rather than "old-fashioned respect" is ex-emplified in the following anecdote of young America. A Professor of Ped-agogy in a Western university brings up his children on the most advanced principles. Among other things, they are encouraged to sink the antiquated terms " father " and " mother," and call their parents by their Christian names. On one occasion, the children, playing in the bathroom, turned on the water and omitted to turn it off again. Observing it percolating through the ceiling of his study, their father rushed upstairs to see what was the matter, flung open the bathroom door, and was greeted by the prime mover in the mischief, a boy of six, with the remark, " Don't say a word, John— bring the mop!"

actress. Two daughters, of about eighteen and twenty, respectively, are on the stage, acting in their father's company; but the master of the house is a bright little boy of seven or eight, known as " the Commodore." As it happened, the mother of the family was away for the day; yet in the hundred affectionate references made to her by the father and daughters, not to me, but to each other, I read her character and influence more clearly, perhaps, than if she had been present in the flesh. A more simple, natural, unaffectedly beautiful " interior " no novelist could conceive.

If the family tie is seriously relaxed in America, it seems an odd coincidence that I should in a single month have chanced upon two households where it is seen in notable perfection, to say nothing of many others in which it is at least as binding as in the average English home.

POSTSCRIPT.—The American university system is a very large subject, to which none but a specialist could do justice, and that in a volume, not a postscript. Nevertheless I should like slightly to supplement the above allusion to it. In the first place, let me quote from the *Spectator* (February 12, 1898) the following passage:

" Some of the American Universities, in our judgment, come nearer to the ideal of a true University than any of the other types. Beginning on the old English collegiate system, they have broadened out into vast and splendidly endowed institutions of universal learning, have assimilated some German features, and have combined successfully college routine and discipline with mature and advanced work. Harvard and Princeton were originally English colleges; now, without entirely abandoning the college system, they are great semi-German seats of learning. Johns Hopkins at Baltimore is purely of the German type, with no residence and only a few plain lecture rooms, library, and museums. Columbia, originally an old English college (its name was King's, changed to Columbia at the Revolution), is now perhaps the first University in America, magnificently endowed, with stately buildings, and with a school of political and legal science second only to that of Paris. Cornell, intended by its generous founder to be a sort of cheap glorified technical institute, has grown into a great seat of culture. The quadrangles and lawns of Harvard, Yale, and Princeton almost recall Oxford and Cambridge; their lecture-rooms, laboratories, and post-graduate studies hint of Germany where nearly all American teachers of he present generation have been educated "

Some authorities, however, deplore the Germanising of American education. A Professor of Greek, himself trained in Germany, and recognised as one of the foremost of American scholars, confessed to me his deep dissatisfaction with the results achieved in his own teaching. His students did good work on the scientific and philological side, but their relation to Greek literature as literature was not at all what he could desire. This bears out the remark which I heard another authority make, to the effect that American scholarship was entirely absorbed in the counting of accents, and the like mechanical details; while it seems to run counter to the above suggestion that the university system tends to raise the level of culture while lowering the standard of erudition. At the same time there can be no doubt that the immense width of the field covered by university teaching in America must, in some measure, make for " superficial omniscience" rather than for concentration and research. The truth probably is that the system cuts both ways. The average student seeks and finds general culture in his university course, while the born specialist is enabled to go straight to the study he most affects and concentrate upon it.

To exemplify the latitude of choice offered to the American student, let me give a list of the "courses" in English and Literature at Columbia University, New York, extracted from the Calendar for 1898-99 :

RHETORIC AND ENGLISH COMPOSITION

COURSES I.
1. English Composition. Lectures, daily themes, and fortnightly essays. Professor G. R. CARPENTER. Three hours[6] first half-year.

2. English Composition. Essays, lectures, and discussions in regard to style. Professor G. R. CARPENTER. Three hours, second half-year.

3. English Composition, Advanced Course. Essays, lectures, and consultations. Dr. ODELL. TWO hours.

4.Elocution. Lectures and Exercises. Mr. PUTNAM. TWO hours.

5. The Art of English Versification. Professor BRANDER MATTHEWS. *Not given in* 1898-9.]

6. Argumentative Composition. Lectures, briefs, essays, and oral discussions.

Mr. BRODT. Three hours.

[6] That is, three hours a week ; so, too, in all subsequent instances.

7. Seminar. The topics discussed in 1898-9 will be: Canons of rhetorical propriety (first half-year); the teaching of formal rhetoric in the secondary school (second half-year). Professor G. R. CARPENTER.

ENGLISH AND LITERATURE
COURSES

1 and 2. Anglo-Saxon Language and Historical English Grammar. Mr. SEWARD. TWO hours.

3. Anglo-Saxon Literature: Poetry and Prose. Professor JACKSON. TWO hours.

4. Chaucer's Language, Versification, and Method of Narrative Poetry. Professor JACKSON. TWO hours.

[5. English Language and Literature of the Eleventh, Twelfth, and Thirteenth Centuries. Professor PRICE. *Not given in* 1898-9.]

[6. English Language and Literature of the Fourteenth Century, exclusive of Chaucer, and of the Fifteenth Century; Reading of authors, with investigation of special questions and writing of essays. Professor PRICE. *Not given in* 1898-9.]

7. English Language and Literature of the Sixteenth Century ; Reading of authors, with investigation of special questions and writing of essays. Professor JACKSON. TWO hours.

Courses 5, 6, and 7 are designed for the careful study of the language and literature of Early and Middle English Periods; Course 6 was given in 1897-8.

[8. Anglo-Saxon Prose and Historical English Syntax. Investigation of special questions and writing of essays. Professor PRICE. *Not given in* 1898-9. *To be given in* 1899-1900.]

[10. English Verse-Forms: Study of their historical development. Professor PRICE. *Not given in* 1898-9.]

11. History of English Literature from 1789 to the death of Tennyson: Lectures. Professor WOODBERRY. Three hours.

12. History of English Literature from 1660 to 1789: Lectures. Mr. KROBBBR. Three hours.

[13. History of English Literature from the birth of Shakespeare to 1660, with special attention to the origin of the drama in England and to the poems of Spenser and Milton. Professor WOODBERRY. *Not given in* 1898-9.]

Courses 12 and 13 are given in alternate years.

[14. Pope : Language, Versification, and Poetical Method. Professor PRICE. *Not given in* 1898 9.]

15. Shakespeare: Language, Versification, and Method of Dramatic Poetry. Text: Cambridge Text of Shakespeare. Professor JACKSON. TWO hours.

16. American Literature. Professor BRANDER MATTHEWS. Two hours.

[17. The Poetry, Lyrical, Narrative, and Dramatic, of Tennyson, Browning, and Arnold. Professor PRICE. *Not given in* 1898-9.]

LITERATURE
COURSES

1. The History of Modern Fiction. Professor BRANDER MATTHEWS. TWO hours.

2. The Theory, History, and Practice of Criticism, with special attention to Aristotle, Boileau, Lessing, and English and later French writers, and a study of the great works of imagination. Professor WOODBERRY. Three hours.

[3. Epochs of the Drama. Professor BRANDER MATTHEWS. *Not given inc* 1898-9.]

4. Dramatists of the Nineteenth Century. Professor BRANDER MATTHEWS. TWO hours.

5. Moliere and Modern Comedy. Professor BRANDER MATTHEWS. Two hours.

[6. The Evolution of the Essay. Professor BRANDER MATTHEWS. *Not given in* I898-9.]

7. Studies in Literature, mainly Critical: Selected Works, in Prose and Verse, illustrating the Character and Development of National Literatures. Lectures. Professor WOODBERRY. Three hours.

8. Studies in Literature, mainly Historical: Narrative Poetry of the Middle Ages. Lectures and Conferences. Mr. TAYLOR TWO hours.

[9. The Lyrical Poetry of the Middle Ages. Professor G. R. CARPENTER. *Not given in* I898-9.]

10. Hellenism: Its Origin, Development, and Diffusion, with some account of

the Civilisations that preceded it. Lectures and Conferences. Mr. TAYLOR. Three hours.

11. Literary Phases of the Transition from Paganism to Christianity, with il-lustrations from the other Arts of Expression. Lectures and Conferences. Mr. TAY-LOR. One hour.

Seminar in Literature. Professor WOODBBRRY.

Seminar in the History of the Drama. Professor BRANDER MATTHEWS.

A "seminar" is an institution borrowed from Germany. The professor and a small number of students (six or eight at the outside) sit together round a table, with their books at hand, and pass an hour in cooperative study and discussion. In going through the noble library of Columbia University, I came upon an alcove devoted to Scandinavian literature, with a table on which lay some Danish books. The gentle-man who was guiding me round happened to be an instructor in the Scandinavian languages. He pointed to the books and said, " I have just been having a seminar here, in Danish literature." Seeing on the shelves an edition of Holberg, I asked him if he had ever considered the question why Holberg's comedies, so delightful in the original, appeared to be totally untranslatable into English. " One of my students," he said, " put the same question to me only to-day." One could scarcely desire a better example of the all-embracing range of the studies which an American Uni-versity provides for and encourages. I have heard it said, with a sneer, that " You can take an honours degree in Marie Corelli." If you can graduate with honours in Holberg, your time, in so far, has certainly not been misemployed.

Whatever the drawbacks of the German influence which is so marked in America, I cannot doubt that in one thing, at any rate, the Americans are far ahead of us—in the careful study they devote to the science of education. No fewer than twenty courses of lectures on the theory and practice of education were given in Columbia College during 1898-99. Teaching, I take it, is an art founded upon, and intimately associated with, the science of psychology. Why should we be content with antiquated and rule-of-thumb methods, instead of going to the root of the thing, studying its principles, and learning to apply them to the best advantage ?

LETTER VI

Washington in April—A Metropolis in the Making— The White House, the Capitol, and the Library of Congress—The Symbolism of Washington.

WASHINGTON.

To profess oneself disappointed with Washington in this first week of April, 1899, would be like complaining of the gauntness of a rose-bush in December. What would you have ? It is not the season, either politically or atmospherically. Congress is gone, and spring has not come. In the city of leafy avenues there is not a leaf to be seen, and, except the irrepressible crocus, not a flower. A fortnight hence, as I am assured, the capital of the Great Republic will have put on a regal robe of magnolia and other blossoms, that will " knock spots out of" Solomon in all his glory. In the meantime, the trees line the avenues in skeleton rows, like a pyrotechnic set-piece before it is ignited. It is useless to pretend, then, that I have seen Washington. The trumpet of March has blown, the pennon of May is not yet unfurled; and even the cloudless sunshine of the past two days has only reduplicated the skeleton trees in skeleton shadows. Washington is not responsible for the tardiness of the spring. It would be unjust to take umbrage at the city because one finds none in its avenues.

Yet I cannot but feel that I have, so to speak, found Washington out. I have chanced upon her without her make-up, and seen the real face of the city divested of its wig of leafage and rouge of blossoms. Here, for the first time, at any rate, I am impressed by that sense of rawness and incompleteness which is said to be characteristic of America. Washington will one day be a magnificent city, of that there is no doubt; but for the present it is distinctly unfinished. The very breadth of its avenues, contrasted with the comparative lowness of the buildings which line them, gives it the air rather of a magnified and glorified frontier township than of a great capital on the European scale. Here, for the first time, I am really conscious of the newness of things. The eastern cities—Boston, New York, Philadelphia, Baltimore—are, in effect, not a whit newer than most English towns. Oxford and Cambridge, no doubt, and a few cathedral cities, give one a habitual consciousness of dwelling among the relics of the past. They are our Nuremburg or Prague, Siena or Perugia. In most English cities, on the other hand, as in London itself, one has no habitual sense of the antiquity of one's surroundings. Apart from a few tourist-haunted monuments, which the resident passes with scarcely a glance, the general run of buildings and streets, if not palpably modern, can at most lay claim to a respectable, or disreputable, middle-age. Now, an eminently respectable middle-age is precisely the characteristic of the central regions of Philadelphia and Baltimore; while in New York both reputable and disreputable middle age are amply represented. One may almost say that these Eastern cities are fundamentally old-fashioned, and that all their modern mechanism of electric cars, telephone wires, and what not, is but a thin and transparent outer network, through which the older order of things is everywhere peering. And from this very contrast between the old and the new, this sense of visible time-strata in the structure of a city, there results a very real effect of age.

Here, in Washington, one instinctively craves for something of that uniformity which one instinctively deprecates as an ideal for New York. The buildings on the main streets are too haphazard, like the books on an ill-arranged shelf: folios, quartos, and duodecimos huddled pell-mell together. But when some approach to a definite style is achieved, how noble will be the radiating vistas of this spacious city! The plan of the avenues and streets, as has been aptly said, suggests a cart-wheel superimposed upon a gridiron—an arrangement, by the way, which may be studied on a small scale in Carlsruhe. The result is dire bewilderment to the traveller; my bump of locality, usually not ill-developed, seems to shrink into a positive indentation before the problems presented in such formulas as " K Street, corner of 13th Street, N.E." But from the Capitol, whence most of the avenues spread fanwise, the views they offer are superb; and Pennsylvania Avenue, leading to the Government offices and the White House, will one day, undoubtedly, be one of the great streets of the world. For the present its beauty is not heightened by the new Postal

Department, a massive but somewhat forbidding structure in grey granite, which dominates and frowns upon the whole street. From certain points of view it seems almost to dwarf the Washington Obelisk, the loftiest stone structure in the world. It is a pity that this fine monument should be placed in such a low situation, on the very shore of the Potomac. From the central parts of the city it loses much of its effect, but seen from the distance it stands forth impressively.

People are discontented, it would seem, with the White House, and talk of replacing it with a larger and showier edifice. The latter change, at any rate, would be a change for the worse. There could not be a more appropriate and dignified residence for the Chief Magistrate of a republic. On the other hand, one cannot but foresee a gradual enrichment and ennoblement of the interior of the Capitol. Externally it is magnificent, especially now that the side towards the city has been terraced and balustraded; but internally its decorations are quite unworthy of modern America. The floors, the doors, the cornices and mouldings are cheap in material, dingily garish in colour. Especially painful are the crude blue-and-yellow mosaic tiles of the corridors. The mural decorations belong to several artistic periods, all equally debased. On the whole, it is inconceivable that Congress should for long content itself with an abode which, without being venerable, is simply out of date. The main architectural proportions of the interior are dignified enough. What is wanted is merely the transmutation of stucco into marble, painted pine into oak, and pseudo-Italian arabesques into American frescoes and mosaics. Why should Congress itself be more meanly housed than its Library ?

This new Library of Congress is certainly the crown and glory of the Washington of to-day. It is an edifice and an institution of which any nation might justly boast. It is simple in design, rich in material, elaborate, and for the most part beautiful, in decoration. The general effect of the entrance hall and galleries is at first garish, and some details of the decoration will scarcely bear looking into. Yet the building is, on the whole, in fresco, mosaic, and sculpture, a veritable treasure-house of contemporary American art. Even in this clear Southern climate, the effect of gaudiness will in time pass off. Fifty years hence, perhaps, when there are no living susceptibilities to be hurt, some of the less successful panels and medallions may be "hatched over again, and hatched different." But many of the decorations, I am convinced, will prove possessions for ever to the American people. As for the Rotunda Reading Room, it is, I think, almost above criticism in its combination of dignity with splendour. Far be it from me to belittle that great and liberal institution, the British Museum Reading Room. It is considerably larger than this one; it is no less imposing in its severe simplicity; and it offers the serious student a vaster quarry of books to draw upon, together with wider elbow-room and completer accommodations. But the Library of Congress is still more liberal, for it admits all the world without even the formality of applying for a ticket; and it substitutes for the impressiveness of simplicity the allurements of splendour. It is impossible to conceive a more brilliant spectacle than this Rotunda when it is lighted at night by nearly fifteen-hundred incandescent lamps. Nor is it possible for me to describe in this place the mechanical marvels of the institution — the huge underground boiler-house, with its sixteen boilers; the electrician's room, clean and bright as a new dollar, with its " purring dynamos " and its immense switch-board; the tunnel through which books are delivered by electric trolley to the legislators in the Capitol, within eight minutes of the time they are applied for; and, most wonderful of all, the endless chain, with its series of baskets, whereby books are not only brought down to the reading-room, but re-delivered, at the mere touch of a button, on whatever " deck " of the nine-storied " book-stacks " they happen to belong to. So ingenious is this triumph of mechanism that the baskets seem positively to go through complex processes of thought and selection. Talking of thought and selection, by the way, every one connected with the library speaks with enthusiasm of President McKinley's wise and publicspirited choice of the new chief librarian. Mr. Herbert Putnam, late of the Boston Public Library, is the ideal man for the post, and his appointment was made, not only without suspicion of jobbery, but in the teeth of strong political influence. Mr. McKinley's action in this matter is considered to be not only right in itself, but an invaluable precedent.

Let me not be understood, I beg, to make light of the National Capital. I merely say that to the outward eye it is not yet the city it is manifestly destined to become. Its splendid potentialities do some wrong to its eminently spacious and seemly actuality. But to the mind's eye, to the ideal sense, it has the imperishable beauty of absolute fitness. Omniscient Baedeker informs us that when it was founded there was some thought of calling it " Federal City." How much finer, in its heroic and yet human associations, is the name it bears! Since Alfred the Great, the Anglo-Saxon race has produced no loftier or purer personality than George Washington, and his country could not blazon on her shield a more inspiring name. Carlyle's treatment of Washington is, perhaps, the most unpardonable of his many similar offences. One almost wonders at the forgiving spirit in which the decorators of the Library of Congress have inscribed upon the walls of the new building certain maxims from the splenetic Sage. And if the city is named with exquisite fitness, so are its radiating avenues. Each of them takes its name from one of the States of the Union—names which, as Stevenson long ago pointed out, form an unrivalled array of "sweet and sonorous vocables." In its whole conception, Washington is an ideal capital for the United States —not least typical, perhaps, in its factitiousness, since this Republic is not so much a product of natural development as a deliberate creation of will and intelligence. It represents the struggle of an Idea against the crude forces of nature and human nature. The Capitol, with its clear and logical design, is as aptly symbolic of its history and function as are our Houses of Parliament, with their bewildering but grandiose agglomeration of shafts and turrets, spires and pinnacles; and the two buildings should rank side by side in the esteem of the English-speaking peoples, as the twin foci of our civilisation.

LETTER VII

American Hospitality — Instances—Conversation and Story-Telling—Over-Profusion in Hospitality—Expen-siveness of Life in America—The American Barber— Postcript: An Anglo-American Club.

BOSTON.

MUCH has been said of American hospitality; too much cannot possibly be said. Here am I in Boston, the guest of one of the foremost clubs of the city. I sit, as I write, at my bedroom window, with a view over the whole of Boston Common, and the beautiful spires of the Back-Bay region beyond. I step out on my balcony, and the gilded dome of the State House—" the Hub of the Universe "—is but a stone's-throw off. Through the leafless branches of the trees I can see the back of St. Gaudens's beautiful Shaw Monument, and beyond it the graceful dip of upper Beacon Street. My room is as spacious and luxurious as heart can desire, lighted by half a dozen electric lamps, and with a private bath-room attached, which is itself nearly as large as the bedroom assigned me in the "swagger" hotel of New York—an establishment, by the way, of which it has been wittily said that its purpose is " to provide exclusiveness for the masses." All the comforts of the club are at my command; the rooms are delightful, the food and service excellent. In short, I could not be more conveniently or agreeably situated. Of course I pay the club charges for my room and meals, but it is mere hospitality to allow me to do so. And how do I come to be established in these quarters ? The little story is absolutely commonplace, but all the more typical.

In Washington I made the acquaintance of a gentleman who invited me to lunch at the leading diplomatic and social club. I had no claim upon him of any sort, beyond the most casual introduction. He regaled me with little-neck clams, terrapin, and all the delicacies of the season, and invited to meet me half a dozen of the most interesting men in the city, all of them strangers to me until that moment. I found myself seated next an exceedingly amiable man, whose name I had not caught when we were introduced. One of the first things he asked me was—not " What did I think of America ? " no one ever asked me that—but "Where was I going next ? " To Boston. " Where was I going to put up?" I thought of going to the T—Hotel. "Much better go the U—Club," he replied; " I've no doubt they will be able to give you a room. As soon as lunch is over, I shall telegraph to the club and make sure that everything is ready for you." I, of course, thanked him warmly. "But what credentials shall I present?" "You don't require any—just present your card. I shall make it all right for you." This was a man whom I had met ten minutes before, whose name I did not know, and to whom I had been introduced by a man whom I barely knew! It did not appear that he, on his side, knew or cared about anything I had said or done in the world. He simply obeyed the national instinct of courtesy and helpfulness. And he was as good as his word. Arriving in Boston at a somewhat unearthly hour in the morning, I found my room allotted me and the club servants ready to receive me with every attention. I felt like the Prince in the fairy tale, only that I had done nothing whatever to oblige the good fairy.

Another example. I had a letter of introduction to the Governor of one of the States of the Union, probably (what does not always happen) the most universally respected man in the State, and a member of one of its oldest and most distinguished families. I left the letter, with my card, at this gentleman's house, and in the course of a few hours received a note from his wife, telling me that, owing to a death in the family, they were not then entertaining at all, but saying that the Governor would call upon me to offer me any courtesy or assistance in his power. And so he did. He called, not once, but twice. He presented me with a card for one of the leading clubs of the city, and if my time had allowed me to avail myself of his courtesy, he would have put me in the way of seeing any or all of the State institutions to the best advantage. The governorship of an American State, let me add, is no ornamental sinecure. This was not only a man in high position, but a very busy man. Is there any other country where a mere letter of introduction is so generously honoured ? If so, it is to me an undiscovered country.

These are but two cases out of a hundred. The Americans are said to be the busiest people in the world (I have my doubts on that point), but they have always leisure to give a stranger "a good time." Even, be it noted, during the working hours of the day. My evenings being occupied with theatre-going, I could not accept invitations to dinner; wherefore those who were hospitably inclined towards me had to invite me to lunch; and a luncheon party in America invariably absorbs the best part of an afternoon. A score of these delightful gatherings will always remain in my memory. The " bright" American is, to my thinking, the best talker in the world— certainly the best talker in the English language. A light and facile humour, a power of giving ! a pleasant little sparkle even to sufficiently common-place sayings, is in this country the rule and not the exception. I must have met at these luncheon parties, and actually conversed with, at least a hundred different men of all ages and occupations, and I do not remember among them a single dull, pompous, morose, or pedantic person. The parties did not usually exceed six or eight in number, so that there was no necessity for breaking up into groups. The shuttlecock of conversation was lightly bandied to and fro across the round table. Each took his share and none took more. All topics— even the burning question of " expansion "—were touched upon gaily, humorously, and in perfect good temper.

It is said that American conversation among men tends to degenerate into a mere exchange of anecdotes. I can remember only one party which was in the least degree open to this reproach ; and there the anecdotes were without exception so good and so admirably told, that I, for one, should have been sorry to exchange them for even the loftiest discourse on Shakespeare and the musical glasses. Here, for instance, is an example of the American gift of picturesque exaggeration. On board one of the Florida steamboats, which have to be built with exceedingly light draught to get over the frequent shallows of the rivers, an Englishman accosted the captain with the remark, " I understand, captain, that you think nothing of steaming across a meadow where there's been a heavy fall of dew." "Well, I don't know about that," replied the captain, " but it's true we have sometimes to send a man ahead with a watering-pot !" Or take, again, the story of the southern colonel who was conducted to the theatre to see Salvini's Othello. He witnessed the performance gravely, and remarked at the close, " That was a mighty good show, and I don't see but the coon did as well as any of 'em." A third anecdote that charmed me on this occasion was that of the man who, being invited to take a drink, replied, " No, no, I solemnly promised my dear dead mother never to touch a drop; besides, boys, it's too early in the morning; besides, I've just had one! "

Furthermore, as I recall the party in question, I feel that I am wrong in implying that the conversation was mainly composed of anecdotes. It was mainly composed of narratives ; but that is a different matter. There is a clear distinction between the mere story-teller and the narrator. Two or three of the party were brilliant narrators, and delighted us with accounts of personal experiences, quaint character-sketches, novels in a nutshell. One of the guests was, without exception, the most ready-witted man I ever met. His inexhaustible gift of lightning repartee I saw illustrated on another occasion, when he presided at the midnight "gambol" of a Bohemian club, at which it needed the utmost tact and presence of mind to "ride the whirlwind and direct the storm." At the luncheon party, he related several episodes from his chequered journalistic career in a style so easy and yet so graphic that one felt, if they could have been taken down in shorthand, they would have been literature ready-made. It is a clear injustice to confound such talk as this with a mere bandying of Joe-Millers. The one drawback to American hospitality is that it is apt to be too profuse. I have more than once had to offer a mild protest against being entertained by a hard-working brother journalist on a scale that would have befitted a millionaire. The possibility of returning the compliment in kind affords the canny Scot but poor consolation. A dinner three times more lavish and expensive than you want is not sweetened by the thought that you may, in turn, give your host a dinner three times more expensive and lavish than *he* wants. Both parties, on this system, suffer in digestion and in pocket, while only Delmonico is the gainer. It seems to me, on the whole, that in this country the millionaire is too commonly allowed to fix the standard of expenditure. Society would not be less, but more, agreeable if, instead of always emulating the splendours of Lucullus, people now and then studied the art of Horatian frugality. And I note that in club life, if the plutocrat sets the standard of expenditure, the aristocrat looks to the training of the servants. Their obsequiousness is almost painful. There is not the slightest trace of democratic equality in their dress, their manners, or their speech.

Take it all and all, America is a trying place of sojourn for the aforesaid canny Scot—the man who without being stingy (oh, dear, no!) has " all his generous impulses under perfect control." The sixpences do not "bang" in this country: they crepitate, they crackle, as though shot from a Maxim quick-firer. For instance, the lowest electric-trolley fare is twopence-halfpenny. It is true that for five cents you can, if you wish it, ride fifteen or twenty miles; but that advantage becomes inappreciable when you don't want to ride more than half a mile. Take, again, the harmless, necessary operation of shaving. In a good English barber's shop it is a brief and not unpleasant process; in an American "tonsorial parlour" it is a lingering and costly torture. One of the many reasons which lead me to regard the Americans as a leisurely people rather than a nation of "hustlers" is the patience with which they submit to the long-drawn tyranny of the barber. In England one grudges five minutes for a shave, and one pays from fourpence to sixpence; in America one can hardly escape in twenty-five minutes, and one pays (with the executioner's tip) [7] from a shilling to eighteenpence. The charge would be by no means excessive if one wanted or enjoyed all the endless processes to which one is subjected;

> [7] I had read or been told that the tip system did not obtain in America, except in the case of negroes and waiters. A very few days in New York undeceived me. I went twice to a barber's shop in the basement of the house in which I lived, paid fifteen cents to be shaved, and gave the operator nothing; but at my second visit I found myself so lowered upon by that portly and heavy-moustached citizen that I never again ventured to place myself under his razor, but went to a more distant establishment and tipped from the outset. There are, indeed, certain classes of people—railroad conductors for instance—who do not expect the tips which in England they consider their due; but, according to my experience, the safe rule in America is " when in doubt— tip."

but for my part I would willingly pay double to escape them. The essential part of the business, the actual shaving, is, as a rule, badly performed, with a heavy hand, and a good deal of needless pawing-about of the patient's head. But when the shave is over the horrors are only beginning. First, your whole face is cooked for several minutes in relays of towels steeped in boiling water. Then a long series of essences is rubbed into it, generally with the torturer's naked hand. The sequence of these essences varies in different " parlours," but one especially loathsome hell-brew, known as "witch-hazel," is everywhere inevitable. Then your wounds have to be elaborately doctored with stinging chemicals; your hair, which has been hopelessly touzled in the pawing process, has to be drenched in some sickly-smelling oil and brushed; your moustache has to be lubricated and combed; and at last you escape from the tormentor's clutches, irritated, enervated, hopelessly late for an important appointment, and so reeking with unholy odours that you feel as though all great Neptune's ocean would scarcely wash you clean again. Only once or twice have I submitted, out of curiosity, to the whole interminable process. I now cut it short, not without difficulty, before the "witch-hazel" stage is reached, and am regarded with blank astonishment and disapproval by the tonsorial professor, who feels his art and mystery insulted in his person, and is scarcely mollified by a ten-cent tip.

Americans, on the other hand, go through all these processes, and more, with stolid and long-suffering patience. Yet this nation is credited with having invented the maxim "Time is money," and is supposed to act up to it with feverish consistency!

POSTSCRIPT.—As I have said a good deal about clubs in this letter, let me add to it a word as to the influence of club life in keeping America in touch with England. At all the leading clubs one or two English daily papers and all the more important weekly papers are taken as a matter of course; so that the American club-man has not the slightest difficulty in keeping abreast of the social, political, and literary life of England. As a matter of fact, the educated American's knowledge of England every day puts to shame the Englishman's ignorance of America. Reciprocity in this matter would be greatly to the advantage of both countries. I am much mistaken if there is a single club in London where American periodicals are so well represented on the reading-room table as are English periodicals in every club in New York. Yet there is assuredly no dearth of interesting weekly papers in America, some connected with daily papers, others independent. It may be said that they are not taken at English clubs because they would not be read. If so, the mores the pity; but I do not think it is so; for this is a case in which supply would beget demand. At any rate,- there must be numbers of people in London who would be glad to keep fairly in touch with American life, if they could do so without too much trouble. Why should there not be an Anglo-American social club, organised with the special purpose of bringing America home (in a literal sense) to London and England ? Why should not (say) the Century Club of New York be reproduced in London, with American periodicals as fully represented in its news-room and reading-room as are English periodicals in an American club of the first rank ? Interest in and sympathy with America would be the implied condition of membership; and by a judiciously-devised system of non-resident membership, American visitors to London would be enabled to read their home newspapers in greater comfort than at the existing American reading-rooms, and would, moreover, come into easy contact with sympathetically-minded Englishmen, to their mutual pleasure and profit. Such a club might, in process of time, become a potent factor in international relations, and form a new bond of union, of quite appreciable strength, between the two countries.

LETTER VIII

Boston — Its Resemblance to Edinburgh — Concord, Walden Pond, and Sleepy Hollow—ls the " Yankee " Dying Out?—America for the Americans—Detroit and Buffalo—The ' Middle West."

CHICAGO.

THE luxury of my quarters in Boston seduced me into a disquisition on American hospitality which would have come in equally well with reference to any other city. Were I to search very deeply into my soul (an exercise much in vogue in Boston), I might perhaps find reasons for my rambling off. To say that Boston did not interest me would be the reverse of the truth. It interested me deeply; but it did not excite me with a sense of novelty or vastness. One can only repeat the obvious truth that it is like an exceptionally dignified and stately English town. One instinctively looks around for a cathedral, and finds the State House in its stead. To the founders of this city, the glory of God was not a thing to be furthered, or even typified, by any work of men's hands; but the salvation of men's souls, they thought, could be best achieved in a well-ordered democratic polity. Their descendants have of late years taken to decorating their places of worship, and Trinity Church (by H. H. Richardson), and the new Old South Church, are ambitious and beautiful pieces of ecclesiastical architecture. But the old Old South Meeting-House, the ecclesiastical centre of the city, is the flat and somewhat sour negation of all that is expressed or implied in an English cathedral. Let me not be understood to disparage the Old South or the spirit which fashioned it. In my eyes, minster and meetinghouse are equally interesting historic monuments, and to my hereditary instincts the latter is the more sympathetic. I merely note the fact that the most conspicuous edifice in Boston, its Duomo, its St. Peter's or St. Paul's, is dedicated, not to the glory of God, but to the well-being of man.

Not physically, of course, but intellectually, Boston has been likened to Edinburgh. The parallel is fair enough, with this important reservation, that the theological element in the atmosphere is not Presbyterian but Unitarian. The Boston of today, it must be added, especially resembles Edinburgh in the fact that its pre-eminence as an intellectual centre has virtually departed. The ***Atlantic Monthly*** survives, as ***Blackwood survives,*** a relic of the great days of old; but Boston has no Scott Monument to bear visual testimony to her spiritual achievement. She ought certainly to treat herself to a worthy Emerson Monument on the Common, whither the boy Emerson used to drive his mother's cows: not, of course, a Gothic pile like that which commemorates the genius of Scott, but a statue by the incomparable St. Gaudens, under a modest classic canopy.

But if, or when, such a monument is erected, it will absolve no one of the duty of making a pilgrimage to Concord. Even if it had no historic or literary associations, this simple, dignified, beautiful New England village, with its plain frame houses and its stately elm avenues, would be well worth a visit. Village I call it, but township would be a better word. Let no one go there with less than half a day to spare, for the places of interest are widely scattered. My companion and I went first to Walden Pond, then to the Emerson and Hawthorne houses, then to that ideal burying-place, Sleepy Hollow, where Emerson and Hawthorne and Thoreau rest side by side, and finally to the bridge—

Where once the embattled farmers stood,
And fired the shot heard round the world.

Everything here is beautifully appropriate. The commemorative statue of the "minute-man" with his musket is simple and expressive, and the four lines of Emerson's hymn graven on the pedestal are the right words written by the right man, entwining, as it were, the historical and literary associations of the place. An exquisite appropriateness, too, presides over the Poets' Corner of Sleepy Hollow. The grave of Emerson is marked by a rough block of pure white quartz, in which is inserted a bronze tablet bearing the words:

The passive master lent his hand

To the vast soul that o'er him planned.

Altogether, among the places of pilgrimage of the English-speaking race, there is none more satisfac-factory or more inspiring than Concord, Mass.

If Boston is no longer a great centre of literary production, it remains, with its noble public library in its midst, and with Harvard University on its outskirts, a great centre of culture. I shall always remember a luncheon party at Harvard, where I was the guest of an eminent Shakespearean critic, and had for my fellow guests a very learned Dante scholar (one of the most delightful talkers imaginable), a famous psychologist, a political economist, and a lecturer on English literature. The talk fell upon the depopulation of New England, or rather the substitution of an alien race for (I had almost said) the indigenous Yankee stock. There was some discussion as to whether the Yankee was really dying out, or had merely spread throughout the West, taking with him and disseminating the qualities which had made the greatness of New England. It was not denied, of course, that westward emigration has much to do with the matter. The New England farmer, unable to stand up against the competition of the prairies, has betaken himself to the prairies so as to compete on the winning side. But one of the company maintained that this did not account for the whole phenomenon. " The real key to it," he said, " lies in such a family history as mine. My grandmother was the youngest of thirteen children; my mother was the eldest of five; my brother and I are two; and we are unmarried."

I am inclined to think that this story of a dwindling stock is typical, not for New England alone, but for other parts of the Union. It seems as though the pressure of life in the Eastern States, and perhaps some subtle influence of climate upon temperament, were rendering the people of old Teutonic blood— British, Dutch, and German—unwilling to face the responsibility of large families, and so were giving the country over to the later and usually inferior immigrant and his progeny. I am not sure that it might not be well to cultivate a new sense of social duty in this matter. Is it Utopian to suggest a policy of "America for the Americans"—some effectual restriction of immigration before it is too late, so as to leave room for the natural increase of the American people? This is an "expansion," a " taking up of the white man's burden," which would command my wannest sympathy. It is to the interest of the whole world that the America of the future should be peopled by " white men " in every sense of the word.

New England, however, cannot be utterly depopulated of its old stocks, for at every turn you come up against those good old Puritan names which bespeak a longer ancestry than many an English peer can claim. I find among the signatures to a petition against the reinstatement of an elevated railroad in Boston, such names as Adams, Morse, Lowell, Emerson, Bowditch, Lothrop, Storey, Dabney, Whipple, Ticknor, and Hale. Of the fifty signatures, only three (or, at the outside five, if we include two doubtful cases) are of other than English origin. In contrast to this I may mention another list of names which came under my notice at the same time—a list of the purchasers at a sale by auction of seats for a New York first-night. Here twenty-six names out of forty are obviously of non-English origin, while several of the remaining fourteen have a distinctly Hebraic ring.

Though very much smaller than New York, Chicago, and Philadelphia, Boston is essentially a great city, with a very animated street life, and nothing in the least provincial about it. But it is not in these great capitals, not even in this marvellous Chicago where I am now writing, that one most clearly realises the bewildering potentialities of the United States. It is precisely in the minor, the provincial cities, which to us in Europe are no more than names—perhaps not so much. For instance, what does the average Englishman know of Detroit?[8]

> [8] My own visit to Detroit illustrated this vagueness of the average Eng-
> lishman. I was anxious to see Mr. James A. Heme's famous play, ***Shore***
> ***Acres,*** and learned from Mr. Herne that it would be played by a travelling
> company at

What State is it in? Is it in the North or the South, the East or the West? For my part I knew in a general way, having been there before, that Detroit was situated somewhere between Chicago and Niagara Falls, but until a few days ago I should have been puzzled to describe its situation more precisely. Well, I arrive in this obscure, insignificant place, and find it a city of considerably more than a quarter of a million inhabitants, beautifully laid out, magnificently paved and lighted, its broad and noble avenues lined with handsome commercial houses and roomy if not always beautiful villas, trees shading its sidewalks, electric cars swimming in an endless stream along its bustling thorough-fares, its imposing public library swarming with readers, its theatres crowded, its parks alive with bicyclists, an eager activity, whether in business, culture, or recreation, manifesting itself on every hand. Or take, again, Buffalo, somewhat larger than Detroit, but still by no means a city of the first rank. Everything that I have said of Detroit applies to it, with the addition that some of its commercial buildings are not only palatial in their dimensions, but original and impressive in their architecture. An

Buffalo on a certain date. I carefully noted the place and day, but contrived to mix up Buffalo and Detroit in my mind, and arrived on the appointed day in Detroit—nearly two hundred and fifty miles from the appointed place! It was as though, having arranged to be in Brighton at a certain time, one should go instead to Scarborough.

afternoon stroll along Woodward Avenue, Detroit, or Main Street, Buffalo, reassures one as to the future—the physical future, at any rate—of the American people. The prevailing type is, if not definitely Anglo-Saxon, at any rate Teutonic, and the average of physical development is very high, especially among the women. It may have some bearing upon what I have been saying above to note that, in point of stature and beauty, the Bostonian woman, as a rule, seemed to me to fall far short of her sisters in the other cities I have visited. I have before my mind's eye many distinguished and delightful exceptions to this rule; but, postponing gallantry to sociological candour, I state my general impression for what it is worth.

Here, in Chicago, gallantry and candour go hand in hand. A legend of the envious East represents that a Chicago young man travelling in Louisiana wrote to his sweetheart: " DEAR MAMIE,—I have shot an alligator. When I have shot another I will send you a pair of slippers." The implication is, to the best of my knowledge and belief, a base and baseless calumny. New York itself does not present a higher average of female beauty than Chicago, and that is saying a great deal. But I must not enlarge on this fascinating topic. A Judgment of Paris is always a delicate business, and I am in nowise called upon to make the invidious award. Were I compelled to undertake it, I could only distribute the apple, and my homage, in equal shares to the goddesses of the East, the South, and the Middle West.

When I was in Chicago in '77, it was the metro-" polis of the West, without qualification. Now it is merely the frontier city of the Middle West. From the standpoint of Omaha and Denver, it seems to fill the Eastern horizon, and shut out the further view. Many stories are told to show how absolutely and instinctively your true Westerner ignores the Eastern States and cities. Here is one of the most characteristic. A little girl came into the smoking-car of a train somewhere in Kansas or Nebraska, and stood beside her father, who was in conversation with another man. The father put his arm round her and said to his companion, " She's been a great traveller, this little girl of mine. She's only ten years old, and she's been all over the United States."

" You don't say !" replied the other; " all over the United States ? "

" Yes, sir; all over the United States," said the proud father; and then added, as though the detail was scarcely worth mentioning, "except east of Chicago."

Chicago, unfortunately, marks the limit of my wanderings; so I shall return to England without having seen anything of the United States, except for a sort of Pisgah-glimpse from the tower of the Auditorium.

LETTER IX

Chicago—Its Splendour and Squalor—Mammoth Buildings—Wind, Dust, and Smoke—Culture—Chicago's Self-Criticism—Postcript: Social Service in America.

CHICAGO.

WHEN I was in America twenty-two years ago, Chicago was the city that interested me least. Coming straight from San Francisco—which, in the eyes of a youthful student of Bret Harte, seemed the fitting metropolis of one of the great realms of romance—I saw in Chicago the negation of all that had charmed me on the Pacific slope. It was a flat and grimy abode of mere commerce, a rectilinear Glasgow; and to an Edinburgh man, or rather boy, no comparison could appear more damaging. How different is the impression produced by the Chicago of to-day ! In 1877 the city was extensive enough, indeed, and handsome to boot, in a commonplace, cast-iron fashion. It was a chequer-board of Queen Victoria Streets. To-day its area is appalling, its architecture grandiose. It is the young giant among the cities of the earth, and it stands but on the threshold of its destiny. It embraces in its unimaginable amplitude every extreme of splendour and squalor. Walking in Dearborn Street or Adams Street of a cloudy afternoon, you think yourself in a frowning and fuliginous city of Dis, piled up by superhuman and apparently sinister powers. Cycling round the boulevards of a sunny morning, you rejoice in the airy and spacious greenery of the Garden City. Driving along the Lake Shore to Lincoln Park in the flush of sunset, you wonder that the dwellers in this street of palaces should trouble their heads about Naples or Venice, when they have before their very windows the innumerable laughter, the ever-shifting opalescence, of their fascinating inland sea. Plunging in the electric cars through the river subway, and emerging in the West Side, you realise that the slums of Chicago, if not quite so tightly packed as those of New York or London, are no whit behind them in the other essentials of civilised barbarism. Chicago, more than any other city of my acquaintance, suggests that antique conception of the underworld which placed Elysium and Tartarus not only on the same plane, but, so to speak, round the corner from each other.

As the elephant (or rather the megatherium) to the giraffe, so is the colossal business block of Chicago to the sky-scraper of New York. There is a proportion and dignity in the mammoth buildings of Chicago which is lacking in most of those which form the jagged sky-line of Manhattan Island. For one reason or another— no doubt some difference in the system of land tenure is at the root of the matter— the Chicago architect has usually a larger plot of ground to operate on than his New York colleague, and can consequently give his building breadth and depth as well as height. Before the lanky giants of the Eastern metropolis, one has generally to hold one's aesthetic judgment in abeyance. They are not precisely ugly, but still less, as a rule, can they be called beautiful. They are simply astounding manifestations of human energy and heaven-storming audacity. They stand outside the pale of aesthetics, like the Eiffel Tower or the Forth Bridge. But in Chicago proportion goes along with mere height, and many of the business houses are, if not beautiful, at least aesthetically impressive — for instance, the grim fortalice of Marshall, Field & Company, the Masonic Temple, the Women's Temperance Temple (a structure with a touch of real beauty), and such vast cities within the city as the Great Northern Building and the Monadnock Block. The last-named edifice alone is said to have a daily population of 6000. A city ordinance now limits the height of buildings to ten storeys; but even that is a respectable allowance. Moreover, it is found that where giant constructions cluster too close together, they (literally) stand in each other's light, and the middle storeys do not let. Thus the heaven-storming era is probably over; but there is all the more reason to feel assured that the business centre of Chicago will ere long be not only grandiose but architecturally dignified and satisfactory. A growing thirst for beauty has come upon the city, and architects are earnestly studying how to assuage it. In magnificence of internal decoration, Chicago can already challenge the world: for instance, in the white marble vestibule and corridors of The Rookery, and the noble hall of the Illinois Trust Bank.

At the same time, no account of the city scenery of Chicago is complete without the admission that the gorges and canyons of its central district are exceedingly draughty, smoky, and dusty. Even in these radiant spring days, it fully acts up to its reputation as the Windy City. This peculiarity renders it probably the most convenient place in the world for the establishment of a Suicide Club on the Stevensonian model. With your eyes peppered with dust, with your ears full of the clatter of the Elevated Road, and with the prairie breezes playfully buffeting you and waltzing with you by turns, as they eddy through the ravines of Madison, Monroe, or Adams Street, you take your life in your hand when you attempt the crossing of State Street, with its endless stream of rattling waggons and clanging trolley-cars. New York does not for a moment compare with Chicago in the roar and bustle and bewilderment of its street life. This remark will probably be resented in New York, but it expresses the settled conviction of an impartial pedestrian, who has spent a considerable portion of his life during the past few weeks in " negotiating " the crossings of both cities.

On the other hand, I observe no eagerness on the part of New York to contest the supremacy of Chicago in the matter of smoke. In this respect the eastern metropolis is to the western as Mont Blanc to Vesuvius. The smoke of Chicago has a peculiar and aggressive individuality, due, I imagine, to the natural clearness of the atmosphere. It does not seem, like London smoke, to permeate and blend with the air. It does not overhang the streets in a uniform canopy, but sweeps across and about them in gusts and swirls, now dropping and now lifting again its grimy curtain. You will often see the vista of a gorge-like street so choked with a seeming thundercloud that you feel sure a storm is just about to burst upon the city, until you look up at the zenith and find it smiling and serene. Again and again a sudden swirl of smoke across the street (like that which swept across Fifth Avenue when the Windsor Hotel burst into flames) has led me to prick up my ears for a cry of " Fire!" But Chicago is not so easily alarmed. It is accustomed to having its airs from heaven blurred by these blasts from hell. I know few spectacles more curious than that which awaits you when you have shot up in the express elevator to the top of the Auditorium tower —on the one hand, the blue and laughing lake, on the rther, the city belching volumes of smoke from its thousand throats, as though a vaster Sheffield or Wolverhampton had been transported by magic to the shores of the Mediterranean Sea. What a wonderful city Chicago will be when the commandment is honestly enforced which declares, "Thou shalt consume thine own smoke!"

What a wonderful city Chicago will be! That is the ever-recurring burden of one's cogitations. For Chicago is awake, and intelligently awake, to her destinies; so much one perceives even in the reiterated complaints that she is asleep. Discontent is the condition of progress, and Chicago is not in the slightest danger of relapsing into a condition of inert self-complacency. Her sons love her, but they chasten her. They are never tired of urging her on, sometimes (it must be owned) with most unfilial objurgations; and she, a quite unwearied Titan, is bracing up her sinews for the great task of the coming century. I have given myself a rendezvous in Chicago for 1925, when air-ships will no doubt make the transit easy for my septuagenarian frame. Nowhere in the world, I am sure, does the " to be continued in our next" interest take hold on one with such a compulsive grip.

Culture is pouring into Chicago as rapidly as pork or grain, and Chicago is insatiate in asking for more. In going over the Public Library (a not quite satisfactory building, though with some beautiful details) I was most of all impressed by the army of iron-bound boxes which are perpetually speeding to and fro between the library itself and no fewer than fifty-seven distributing stations scattered throughout the city. " I thought the number was forty-eight," said a friend who accompanied me. " So it was last year," said the librarian. " We have set up nine more stations during the interval." The Chicago Library boasts (no doubt justly) that it circulates more books than any similar institution in the world. Take, again, the University of Chicago: seven years ago (or, say, at the outside ten) it had no existence, and its site was a dismal swamp; to-day it is a handsome and populous centre of literary and scientific culture. Observe, too, that it is by no means an oasis in the desert, but is thoroughly in touch with the civic life around it. For instance, it actively participates in the admirable work done by the Hull House Settlement in South Halsted Street, and in the vigorous and wide-spreading University Extension movement.

At the present moment Chicago is not a little resentful of the sharp admonitions addressed to her by two of her aforesaid loving but exacting children. One, Professor Charles Zueblin, has been telling her that " in the arrogance of youth she has failed to realise that instead of being one of the progressive cities of the world, she has been one of the reckless, improvident, and shiftless cities." Professor Zueblin is not content (for example) with her magnificent girdle of parks and boulevards, but calls for smaller parks and breathing spaces in the heart of her most crowded districts. He further maintains that her great new sewage canal is a gigantically costly blunder; and indeed one cannot but sympathise with the citizens of St. Louis in inquiring by what right Chicago converts the Mississippi into her main sewer. But if Professor Zueblin chastises Chicago with whips, Mr. Henry B. Fuller, it would seem, lashes her with scorpions. Mr. Fuller is one of the leading novelists of the city—for Chicago, be it known, had a flourishing and characteristic literature of her own long before Mr. Dooley sprang into fame. The author of *The Cliff-Dwellers* is alleged to have said that the Anglo-Saxon race was incapable of art, and that in this respect Chicago was pre-eminently Anglo-Saxon. " Alleged," I say, for reports of lectures in the American papers are always to be taken with caution, and are very often as fanciful as Dr. Johnson's reports of the debates in Parliament. The reporter is not generally a shorthand writer. He jots down as much as he conveniently can of the lecturer's remarks, and pieces them out from imagination. Thus, I am not at all sure what Mr. Fuller really said; but there is no doubt whatever of the indignation kindled by his diatribe. Deny her artistic capacities and sensibilities, and you touch Chicago in her tenderest point. Moreover, Mr. Fuller's onslaught encouraged several other like-minded critics to back him up, so that the city has been writhing under the scourges of her epigrammatists. I have before me a letter to one of the evening papers, written in a tone of academic sarcasm which proves that even the supercilious and " donnish " element is not lacking in Chicago culture. "I know a number of artists," says the writer, " who came to Chicago, and after staying here for a while, went away and achieved much success in New York, London, and Paris. The appreciation they received here gave them the impetus to go elsewhere, and thus brought them fame and fortune." Whatever foundation there may be for these jibes, they are in themselves a sufficient evidence that Chicago is alive to her opportunities and responsibilities. She is, in her own vernacular, " making culture hum." Mr. Fuller, I understand, reproached her with her stockyards—an injustice which even Mr. Bernard Shaw would scarcely have committed. Is it the fault of Chicago that the world is carnivorous ? Was not " Nature red in tooth and claw " several aeons before Chicago was thought of ? I do not understand that any unnecessary cruelty is practised in the stockyards; and apart from that, I fail to see that systematic slaughter of animals for food is any more disgusting than sporadic butchery. But of the stockyards I can speak only from hearsay. I shall not go to see them. If I have any spare time, I shall rather spend it in a second visit to St. Gaudens's magnificent and magnificently placed statue of Abraham Lincoln, surely one of the great works of art of the century, and one of the few entirely worthy monuments ever erected to a national hero.

POSTSCRIPT.—The above-mentioned Hull House Settlement in South Halsted Street, under the direction of Miss Jane Addams, is probably the most famous institution of its kind in America; but it is only one of many. There is no more encouraging feature in American life than the zeal, energy, and high and liberal intelligence with which social service of this sort is being carried on in all the great cities. This is a line of activity on which England and America are advancing hand in hand, and however much one may deplore the necessity for such work, one cannot but see in the common impulse which prompts and directs it a symptom of the deep-seated unity of the two peoples. Nothing I saw in America impressed me more than the thorough practicality as well as the untiring devotion which was apparent in the work carried on by Miss Addams in Chicago and Miss Lillian D. Wald in Henry Street, New York. And in both Settlements I recognised the same atmosphere of culture, the same spirit of plain living, hard working, and high thinking, that characterises the best of our kindred institutions in England.

A lady connected with the University of Chicago, who is also a worker at the Hull House Settlement, told me a touching little story which illustrates at once the need for such work in Chicago, and the unexpected response with which it sometimes meets. She had been talking about the beauties of nature to a group of women from the slums, and at the end of her address one of her hearers said, " I aunt never been outside of Chicago, but I know it's true what the lady says. There's two vacant lots near our place, an' when the spring comes, the colours of them —they fair makes you hold your breath. An' then there's the trees on the Avenoo. An' then there's **all** the sky." On another occasion the same lady met with an " unexpected response " of a different order. She was showing a boy from the slums some photographs of Italian pictures, when they came upon a Virgin and Child. " Ah," said the boy at once, " that's Jesus an' His Mother : I alius knows **them** when I sees 'em." "Yes," said Miss R— "there is a purity and grandeur of expression about them, isn't there—" "'Taint that," interrupted the boy, " it's the rims round their heads as gives 'em away!"

Apart from the Settlements, there are many energetically-conducted societies in America for the social and political enlightenment of the masses. I have before me, for instance, a little bundle of most excellent leaflets issued by the League for Social Service of New York. They deal with such subjects as ***The Duties of American Citizenship, The Value of a Vote, The Duty of Public Spirit, The Co-operative City,***. They include an admirable abstract in twenty-four pages of ***Laws Concerning the Welfare of Every Citizen of New York,*** and the same Society issues similar abstracts of the laws of other States. They have a large and well-equipped lecture organisation, and they issue excellent practical ***Suggestions for Conferences and Courses of Study***. The problem to be grappled with by this Society and others working on similar lines is no doubt one of immense difficulty. It is nothing less than the education in citizenship of the most heterogeneous, polyglot, and in some respects ignorant and degraded population ever assembled in a single city since the days of Imperial Rome. The spread of political enlightenment in New York and other cities cannot possibly be very rapid; but no effort is being spared to accelerate it. I sometimes wonder whether the obvious necessity for political education in America may not, in the long run, prove a marked advantage to her, as compared, for instance, with England. Dissatisfaction, as I have said above, is the condition of progress. We are apt to assume that every Briton is born a good citizen; and in the lethargy begotten of that assumption, it may very well happen that we let the Americans outstrip us in the march of enlightenment.

LETTER X

New York in Spring—Central Park—New York not an Ill-governed City—
The United States Post Office— The Express System—Valedictory.

NEW YORK.

IT is with a curious sensation of home-coming that I find myself once more in New York. Spring has arrived before me. The blue dome of sky has lost its crystalline sparkle, and the trees in Madison Square have put on a filmy veil of green. Going to a luncheon party in the Riverside region, I determine, for the sheer pleasure and exhilaration of the thing, to walk the whole way, up Fifth Avenue and diagonally across Central Park. What a magnificent pleasure ground, vast, various, and seductive! A peerless emerald on the finger of Manhattan! If I were not bound by solemn oaths to present myself at West-End Avenue at half-past one, I could loaf all the afternoon by the superb expanse of the Croton Reservoir, looking out over the giant city of sunshine, with the white dome of Columbia College and the pyramid of Grant's Monument on the northern horizon, and far to the eastward the low hills of Long Island.

Passing the Metropolitan Museum of Art, I am reminded, not only that I have never been inside it, but that in all the cities I have visited I have not gone to a single show-place, museum, or picturegallery, save one remarkable private collection in Baltimore. Of course I must also except (a large exception!) the public libraries of Washington, Boston, and Chicago, which are, in a very eminent sense, "showplaces." Still, it seems somewhat remarkable (does it not?) that in a country which is understood in Europe to be monotonous and unattractive to travellers, I should have spent two months not only of intellectual interest but of aesthetic enjoyment, without once, except in a chance moment of idleness, feeling the least inclination to fall back upon the treiasures of European art which it undoubtedly contains. I have even ignored the marvels of nature. I passed within twenty miles of Niagara; I saw the serried icefloes sweeping down from Lake Erie to the cataract; and I did not go to see them plunge over. In the first place, I had been there before; in the second place, I should have had to sacrifice six hours of Chicago, where I wanted, not six hours less, but six weeks more.

Before saying farewell—a fond farewell!—to New York, let me supplement my first impressions with my last. The most maligned of cities I called it; and truly I said well. Here is even the judicious Mr. J. F. Muirhead of " Baedeker," betrayed by his passion for antithesis into describing New York as " a lady in ball costume, with diamonds in her ears and her toes out at her boots." This was written, to be sure, in 1890, and may have been true in its day; for it takes an American city much less than a decade to belie a derogatory epigram. Now, at any rate, New York has had her shoes mended to some purpose. She is not the best paved city in the world, or even in America, but neither is she by any means the worst; and her splendid system of electric and elevated railroads renders her more independent of paving than any European city. Fifth Avenue is paved to perfection; Broadway and Sixth Avenue are not; but at any rate the streets are not for ever being hauled up and laid down again, like some of our leading London thorough-fares. Holborn, for example, may be ideally paved on paper, but its roadway is subject to such incessant eruptions of one sort or another that it is in practice a much more uncomfortable thoroughfare than any of the New York avenues. For the rest, New York has a copious and excellent water supply, which London has not; it has a splendidly efficient fire-brigade ; it has an admirable telephone system, with underground wires; and even its electric trolleys get their motive-power from underneath, whereas in Philadelphia the overhead wires are, I regret to say, killing the trees which lend the streets their greatest charm. Altogether, Tammany or no Tammany, New York cannot possibly be described as an ill governed city. Its government may be wasteful and worse; inefficient it is not. Even the policemen seem to me maligned. I never found them rude or needlessly dictatorial.

In one of the essential conveniences of modern life, New York is far behind London; but the blame lies, not with the city, but with the United States. Its postal arrangements are at best erratic, at worst miserable. Letters which would be delivered in London in three or four hours take in New York anywhere from six to sixteen hours. It was a long time before I realised and learned to allow for the slowness of the postal service. At first I used mentally to accuse my correspondents of great dilatoriness in attending to notes that called for an immediate reply. On one occasion I posted in Madison Square at 3 P.M. a letter addressed to the Lyceum Theatre, not a quarter of a mile away, suggesting an appointment for the same evening after the play. The appointment was not kept, for the letter was not delivered till the following morning! To ensure its delivery the same evening, I ought to have put a special-delivery stamp on it— price fivepence—in addition to the ordinary two-cent stamp. No doubt it is the universal employment of the telephone in American cities that leads people to put up with such defective postal arrangements.

But it is not only within city limits that the United States Post Office functions with a dignified deliberation. The ordinary time that it takes to write (say) from New York to Chicago, and receive an answer, might be considerably reduced without any acceleration of the train service. It sounds incredible, but it is, I believe, the case, that the simple and eminently time-saving device of a letter-box in the domestic front-door is practically unknown in America. I did observe one, in Boston, so small that a fair sized business letter would certainly have stuck in its throat. One evening I was sitting at dinner in a fashionable street in New York, close to Central Park, when I was startled by a distinctly burglarious noise at the window. My host smiled at my look of bewilderment, and explained that it was only the letter-carrier; and, sure enough, when the servant came into the room she picked up three or four letters from the floor. The postman was somehow able to reach the front window from the "stoop," open it, and throw in the evening's mail—a primitive arrangement, more suggestive of the English than of the American Gotham. Even the gum on the United States postage-stamps is apt to be ineffectual. When you are stamping letters in hot haste to catch the European mail, you are as likely as not to find that the head of President Grant has curled up and refuses—most uncharacteristically—to stick to its post.

The conveniences of the express system, again, are, in my judgment, greatly overrated. It is often slow and always expensive. It seems to have been devised by the makers of Saratoga trunks, for it puts a premium upon huge packages and a tax upon those of moderate size. I speak feelingly, for I have just paid eight shillings for the conveyance of five packages from my room to the wharf, a distance of about a mile and a half. A London growler would have taken them and myself to boot for eighteenpence, three of the packages going outside, and two, with their owner, inside. It is true that had I packed all my belongings in one huge box the same company would have conveyed them to the steamer for one and eightpence, which is the regular charge per package. But I could not have taken this box into my state-room; I must in any case have had a cabin trunk; and for an ocean voyage, a bundle of rugs is, to say the least of it, advisable. Thus I could not have escaped paying four and tenpence for the conveyance of my baggage alone— rather more than three times as much as it would have cost to convey my baggage and myself the same distance in London. It must not be forgotten, of course, that the New York Express Company would, if necessary, have carried the goods much further for the same charge of forty cents a package. The limit of distance I do not know: it is probably something like twenty miles. But a potential ell does not reconcile me to paying an exorbitant price for the actual inch which is all I have any use for. This method of simplification—fixing the minimum payment on the basis of the maximum bulk, weight, and distance—seems to me essentially irrational. In some cases, indeed, it cuts against the Express Company. When I first had occasion to move from one abode to another in New York—a distance of about a quarter of a mile—I thought with glee, " Now the famous express system will save me all trouble." But I found that it would cost two dollars to express my belongings, whereas even the notoriously extortionate New York cabman would convey me and all my goods and chattels for half that sum. So the Express Company's loss was cabby's gain.

" The ship is cheered, the harbour cleared," and none too merrily are we dropping down by the Statue of Liberty to Sandy Hook and the Atlantic. (There is a point, by the way, a little below the Battery, from which New York looks mountainous indeed. Its irregularly serrated profile is lost, and the sky-scrapers fall into position one behind the other, like an artistically grouped cohort of giants. " Hills peep o'er hills, and Alps on Alps arise," while in the background the glorious curve of the Brooklyn Bridge seems to span half the horizon. I could not but think of

Valhalla and the Bridge of the Gods in the ***Rheingold.*** Elevator architecture necessarily sends one to Scandinavian mythology in quest of similitudes.) It is with acute regret that I turn my back upon New York, or, rather, turn my face to see it receding over the steamer's wake. Not often in this imperfect world are high anticipations overtopped, as the real America has over topped my half-reminiscent dream of it. " The real America " ? That, of course, is an absurd expression. I have had only a superficial glimpse of one corner of the United States. It is as though one were to glance at a mere dogear on a folio page, and then profess to have mastered its whole import. But I intend no such ridiculous profession. I have seen something of the outward aspect of five or six great cities; I have looked into one small facet of American social life; and I have faithfully reported what I have seen—nothing more. At the same time my observations, and more especially my conversations with the scores of " bright" and amiable men it has been my privilege to meet, have suggested to me certain thoughts, certain hopes and apprehensions, respecting the future of America and the English-speaking world, which I shall try to formulate elsewhere. For the present, let me only sum up my personal experiences in saying that all the pleasant expectations I brought with me to America have been realised, all the forebodings disappointed. Even the interviewer is far less terrible than I had been led to imagine. He always treated me with courtesy, sometimes with comprehension. One gentleman alone (not an American, by the way) set forth to be mildly humorous at my expense; and even he apologised in advance, as it were, by prefixing his own portrait to the interview, as who should say, " Look at me—how can I help it ?" Again, I had been led rather to fear American hospitality as being apt to become importunate and exacting. I found it no less considerate than cordial. Probably I was too small game to bring the lion-hunters upon my trail. The alleged habit of speech-making and speech-demanding on every possible occasion I found to be merely mythical. Three times only was I called upon to " say something," and on the first two occasions, being taken unawares, I said everything I didn't want to say. The third time, having foreseen the demand, I had noted down in advance the heads of an eloquent harangue; but when the time came I felt the atmosphere unpropitious, and suppressed my rhetoric. The proceedings opened with an iced beverage, called, I believe, a "Mississippi toddy," probably as being the longest toddy on record, the father of (fire) waters; and on its down-lapsing current my eloquence was swept into the gulf of oblivion. The meeting, fortunately, did not know what it had lost, and its serenity remained unclouded. But it is not to the Mississippi toddies and other creature comforts of America that I look back with gratitude and affection. It is to the spontaneous and unaffected human kindness that met me on every hand; the will to please and to be pleased in daily intercourse; and, in the spiritual sphere, the thirst for knowledge, for justice, for beauty, for the larger and the purer light.

NORTH AND SOUTH

IN Washington, on the 6th of April last, business was suspended from mid-day onwards, while President McKinley and all the high officers of State attended the public funeral at Arlington Cemetery of several hundred soldiers, brought home from the battlefields of Cuba. The burial ground on the heights of Arling-ton— the old Virginian home, by the way, of the Lee family—had hitherto been known as the resting-place of numbers of Northern soldiers, killed in the Civil War. But among the bodies committed to earth that afternoon were those of many Southern-ers, who had stood and fallen side by side with their Northern comrades at El Caney and San Juan. The significance of the event was widely felt and commented upon. "Henceforth," said one paper, "the graves at Arlington will constitute a truly national cemetery"; and the same note was struck in a thousand other quarters. Poets burst into song at the thought of their

" Resting together side by side,
Comrades in blue and grey !

" Healed in the tender peace of time,
The wounds that once were red
With hatred and with hostile rage,
While sanguined brothers bled.

" They leaped together at the call
Of country—one in one,

The soldiers of the Northern hills
And of the Southern sun!

" ' Yankee' and Rebel,' side by side,
Beneath one starry fold—
To-day, amid our common tears,
Their funeral bells are tolled."

The artlessness of these verses renders them none the less significant. They express a popular sentiment in popular language. But, as here expressed, it is clearly the sentiment of the North : how far is it shared and acknowledged by the South ? Happening to be on the spot, I could not but try to obtain some sort of answer to this question.

Again, as I stood on the terrace of the Capitol that April afternoon, and looked out across the Potomac to the old Lee mansion at Arlington, while all the flags of Washington drooped at half-mast, a very different piece of verse somehow floated into my memory:

" Walk wide o' the Widow at Windsor,
For 'also' Creation she owns:
We have bought ether same with the sword and the flame,
And salted it down with our bones.
(Poor beggars!—it's blue with our bones!)"

The association was obvious: how the price of lead would go up if England brought home all her dead " heroes " in hermetically-sealed caskets! My thought (so an anti-Imperialist might say) was like the smile of the hardened freebooter at the amiable sentimentalism of a comrade who was "yet but young in deed." But why should Mr. Kipling's rugged lines have cropped up in my memory rather than the smoother verses of other poets, equally familiar to me, and equally well fitted to point the contrast ?—for instance, Mr. Housman's:

" It dawns in Asia, tombstones show,
And Shropshire names are read;
And the Nile spills his overflow
Beside the Severn's dead."

Or Mr. Newbolt's:

"Qui procul hiric —the legend's writ,
The frontier grave is far away;
Qui ante diem perilt,
Sed miles, sed pro patria."

The reason simply was that during the month I had spent in America the air had been filled with Kipling. His name was the first I had heard uttered on landing—by the conductor of a horse-car. Men of light and leading, and honourable women not a few, had vied with each other in quoting his refrains; and I had seen the crowded audience at a low music-hall stirred to enthusiasm by the delivery of a screed of maudlin verses on his illness. He, the rhapsodist of the red coat, was out and away the most popular poet in the country of the blue, and that at a time when the blue coat in itself was inimitably popular. Nor could there be any doubt that his **Barrack-room Ballads** were the most popular of his works. Not a century had passed since the Tommy Atkins of that day had burnt the Capitol on whose steps I was standing (a shameful exploit, to which I allude only to point the contrast); and here was the poet of Tommy Atkins so idolised by the grandsons of the men of 1812 and 776, that I, a Briton and a staunch admirer of Kipling, had almost come to resent as an obsession the ubiquity of his name !

It seemed then, that the rancour of the blue coat against the red must have dwindled no less significantly than the rancour of the grey coat against the blue. Into the reality of this phenomenon, too, I made it my business to inquire.

II

THERE can be no doubt that the Spanish War has done a great deal to bring the North and the South together. It has not in any sense created in the South a feeling of loyalty to the Union, but it has given the younger generation in the South an opportunity of manifesting that loyalty to the Union which has been steadily growing for twenty years. Down to 1880, or thereabouts, the wound left by the Civil War was still raw, its inflammation envenomed rather than allayed by the measures of the " reconstruction" period. Since 1880, since the administration of President Hayes, the wound has been steadily healing, until it has come to seem no longer a burning sore, but an honourable cicatrice.

Every one admits that the heaviest blow ever dealt to the South was that which laid Abraham Lincoln in the dust. He, if any one, could have averted the mistakes which delayed by fifteen years the very beginning of the process of reconciliation. His wise and kindly influence removed, the North committed what is now recognised as the fatal blunder of forcing unrestricted negro suffrage on the South. This measure was dictated partly, no doubt, by honest idealism, partly by much lower motives. Then the horde of " carpet-baggers" descended upon the "reconstructed" States, and there ensued a period of humiliation to the South which made men look back with longing even to the sharper agonies of the war. Coloured voters were brought in droves, by their Northern fuglemen, to polling-places which were guarded by United States troops. Utterly illiterate negroes crowded the benches of State legislatures. A Northerner and a staunch Union man has assured me that in the Capitol of one of the reconstructed States he has seen a coloured representative gravely studying a newspaper which he held upside down. The story goes that in the legislature of Mississippi a negro majority, which had opposed a certain bill, was suddenly brought round to it in a body by a chance allusion to its " provisions," which they understood to mean something to eat! This anecdote perhaps lacks evidence; but there can be no doubt that the freedmen of 1865 were, as a body, entirely unfitted to exercise the suffrage thrust upon them. A degrading and exasperating struggle was the inevitable result—the whites of the South striving by intimidation and chicanery to nullify the negro vote, the professional politicians from the North battling, with the aid of United States troops, to render it effectual. Such a state of things was demoralising to both parties, and in process of time the common sense of the North revolted against it. United States troops no longer stood round the ballot-boxes, and the South was suffered, in one way and another, to throw off the " Dominion of Darkness." Different States modified their constitutions in different ways. Many offices which had been elective were made appointive. The general plan adopted of late years has been to restrict the suffrage by means of a very simple test of intelligence, the would-be voter being required to read a paragraph of the State constitution and explain its meaning. The examiner, if one may put it so, is the election judge, and he can admit or exclude a man at his discretion. Thus illiterate whites are not necessarily deprived of the suffrage. They may be quite intelligent men and responsible citizens, who happened to grow to manhood precisely in the years when the war and its sequels upset the whole system of public education in the South. At any rate (it is argued), the illiterate white is a totally different man from the illiterate negro. How far such modifications of the State constitutions are consistent with the Constitution of the United State, is a nice question upon which I shall not attempt to enter. The arguments used to reconcile this test of intelligence with Amendments XIV. and XV. of the United States Constitution seem to me more ingenious than convincing. But, constitutional or not, the compromise is reasonable; and though people in the South still feel, as one of them put it to me, that the Republican party " may yet wield the flail of the negro over them," the flail has been laid aside long enough to permit the South, in the main, to recover its peace of mind and its self-respect. The negro problem is still difficult enough, as many tragic evidences prove; but there is no reason to despair of its ultimate solution.

Meanwhile material prosperity has been returning to the South; agriculture has revived, and manufactures have increased. Social intercourse and intermarriage have done much to promote mutual comprehension between North and South, and to wipe out rankling animosities. Each party has made a sincere effort to understand the other's " case," and the war has come to seem a thing fated and inevitable, or at any rate not to have been averted save by superhuman wisdom and moderation on both sides. With mutual comprehension, mutual admiration has gone hand in hand. The gallantry and tenacity of the South are warmly appreciated in the North, and it is felt on both sides that the very qualities which made the tussle so long and terrible are the qualities which ensure the greatness of the reunited nation. But changes of sentiment are naturally slow and, from moment to moment, imperceptible. It needs some outside stimulus or shock to bring them clearly home to the minds of men. Such a stimulus was provided by the conflict with Spain. It did not create a new sense of solidarity between the North and the South, but rather brought prominently to the surface of the national consciousness a sense of solidarity that had for years been growing and strengthening, more or less obscurely and inarticulately, on both sides of Mason and Dixon's line. It consummated a process of consolidation which had been going on for something like twenty years.

Furthermore, the Spanish War deposed the Civil War from its position as the last event of great external picturesqueness in the national history. However sincere may be our love of peace, war remains irresistibly fascinating to the imagination; and the imagination of young America has now a foreign war instead of a civil war to look back upon. The smoke of battle, in which the South stood shoulder to shoulder with the North, has done more than many years of peace could do to soften in retrospect the harsh outlines of the fratricidal struggle.

At the same time, there is another side to the case which ought not to be overlooked. The South is proud, very proud; and the older generation, the generation which fought and agonised through the terrible years from '61 to '65, is more than a little inclined to resent what it regards as the condescending advances of the North. This feeling is not confined to those out-of-the-way corners where, as the saying goes, they have not yet heard that the war—the Civil War—is over. It is not confined to the old families, ruined by the war, whom the tide of returning prosperity has not reached, and never will reach. It is strong among even the most active and progressive of the veterans of '65. They smile a grim smile in their grizzled beards at the fuss which has been made over this "picayune war," as they call it. They, who came crushed, impoverished, heartbroken, out of the duel of the Titans—they, who know what it really means to sacrifice everything, everything, to a patriotic ideal —they, to whom their cause seems none the less sacred because they know it irrevocably lost—how can they be expected to toss up their caps and help the party which first vanquished, and then, for many bitter years, oppressed them, to make political capital out of what appears, in their eyes, a more or less creditable military picnic ? It is especially the small scale of the conflict that excites their derision. "Did you ever hear of the battle of Dinwiddie Court-House ?" one of them said to me. I confessed that I had not. " No," he said, " nor has any one else heard of the battle of Dinwiddie Court-House. It was one of the most insignificant fights in the war. But there were more men killed in half an hour in that almost forgotten battle than in all this mighty war we hear so much about." " Ah !" he continued, " they think we are vastly gratified when they 'fraternise' with us on our battlefields and decorate the graves of our dead. I don't know but I prefer the ' waving of the bloody shirt' to this flaunting of the olive-branch. They have their victory; let them leave us our graves."

An intense loyalty, not only to the political theories of the South, but to the memory of the men who died for them—"qui bene propatria cum patriaque jacent"—still animates the survivors of the war. With a confessed but none the less pathetic illogicality, they feel as though Death had not gone to work impartially, but had selected for his prey the noblest and the best. One of these survivors, in a paper now before me, quotes from **Das Siegesfest** the line—

" Ja, der Krieg verschlingt die Besten!"

and then remarks: " Still, when Schiller says—

' Denn Patroklus liegt begraben,
Und Thersites kommt zuriick,'

his illustration is only half right. The Greek Thersites did not return to claim a pension."

The dash of bitterness in this remark must not be taken too seriously. The fact remains, however, that among the veterans of the South there prevails a certain feeling of aloofness from the national jubilation over the Spanish War. They "don't take much stock in it." The feeling is widespread, I believe, but not loud-voiced. If I represented it as surly or undignified, I should misrepresent it grossly. It is simply the outcome of an ancient and deep-seated sorrow, not to be salved by phrases or ceremonies— the most tragic emotion, I think, with which I ever came face to face. But it prevails almost exclusively among the older generation in the South, the men who " when they saw the issue of the war, gave up their faith in God, but not their faith in the cause." To the young, or even the middle-aged, it has little meaning. I met a scholar-soldier in the South who had given expression to the sentiment of his race and generation in an essay— one might almost say an elegy—so chivalrous in spirit and so fine in literary form that it moved me well-nigh to tears. Reading it at a public library, I found myself so visibly affected by it that my neighbor at the desk glanced at me in surprise, and I had to pull myself sharply together. Yet the writer of this essay told me that when he gave it to his son to read, the young man handed it back to him, saying, "All this is a sealed book to me. I cannot feel these things as you do."

More important, perhaps, than the sentiment of the veterans is the feeling, which has been pretty generally expressed, that the South was slighted in the actual conduct of the late war—that Southern regiments and Southern soldiers (notably General Fitzhugh Lee) were unduly kept in the background. Still, there is every reason to believe that the general effect of the war has been one of conciliation and consolidation. From the ultra-Southern point of view, the North seems merely to have seized the opportunity of making honourable amends for the "horrors of re-construction"; but even those who take this view admit that the North **has** seized the opportunity, and that gladly. As a matter of fact the goodwill of the North, and its desire to let bygones be bygones, are probably very little influenced by any such recondite motive. It is in most cases quite simple and instinctive. "There are no rebels now," said the commandant of the Brooklyn Navy Yard when he gave orders to delete the fourth word of the inscription "Taken from the rebel ram ***Mississippi*** " over a trophy of the Civil War displayed outside his quarters. Admiral Philips had probably no thought of " reconstruction " or of " making amends "; he simply obeyed a spontaneous and general sentiment. The Southern heroes of the Civil War, moreover, are freely admitted, and enthusiastically welcomed, into the national Pantheon. When the thirty-fourth anniversary of "Appomattox Day," which brought the war to an end, was celebrated in Chicago on April 10 last (Governor Roosevelt being the guest of honour), the memory of Lee was eulogised along with that of Grant, and the oration in his honour was received with equal applause. Finally, it is admitted even by those who are most inclined to make light of the sentiment elicited by the late war, that all the States of the Atlantic seaboard are instinctively drawing together to counterpoise the growing predominance of the West. This substitution of a new line of cleavage for the old one may seem a questionable matter for rejoicing. But in any great community, conflicts of interest must always arise. The recognition of the problems which await the Republic in the near future does not imply any doubt of her ability to arrive at a wise and just solution of them.

III

THE most loyal of the Southern veterans, I have said, recognise that the cause of the South is irrevocably lost. By the cause of the South I do not, of course, mean slavery. There is probably no one in the South who would advocate the reinstatement of that "peculiar institution," even if it could be effected by the lifting of a finger. " The cause we fought for and our brothers died for," says Professor Gildersleeve of Baltimore, " was the cause of civil liberty, not the cause of human slavery. If the secrets of all hearts could have been revealed, our enemies would have been astounded to see how many thousands and tens of thousands in the Southern States felt the crushing burden and the awful responsibility of the institution which we were supposed to be defending with the melodramatic fury of pirate kings."

What was it, then, that the South fought for ? In what sense was its cause the cause of "civil liberty " ? A brief inquiry into this question may be found to have more than a merely historic interest —to have a direct bearing, indeed, upon the problems of the future, not only for America, but for the English-speaking world.

Let me state at once the true inwardness of the matter, as I have been led to see it. The cause of the South was the cause of small against large political aggregations;

and the world regards the defeat of the South as righteous and inevitable, because instinct tells it that the welfare of humanity is to be sought in large political aggregations, and not in small. Providence, in a word, is on the side of the big (social) battalions.

From the point of view of pure logic, of academic argument, the case of the South was enormously strong. Consequently, the latter-day apologists of the Confederacy devote themselves with pathetic fervour, and often with great ingenuity, to what the impartial outsider cannot but feel to be barren discussions of constitutional law. They point out that the States—that is, the thirteen original States—preceded the Federal Union, and voluntarily entered into it under clearly defined conditions; that the Federal Government actually derived its powers from the consent of the States, and could have none which they did not confer upon it; that the maintenance of slavery in the Southern States, and the right to claim the extradition of fugitive slaves, were formally safeguarded in the Constitution; that it was in reliance upon these provisions that the Southern States consented to enter the Union; that the right of secession had been openly and repeatedly asserted by leading politicians and influential parties in several Northern States, and was therefore no novel and treasonable invention of the South; and, finally, that the right to enter into a compact implied the right to recede from it when its provisions were broken, or obviously on the point of being broken, by the other party or parties to the agreement. All this is logically and historically indisputable. The Southerners were the conservative party, and had the letter of the Constitution on their side; the Northerners were the reformers, the innovators. Entrenched in the theory of State Sovereignty, the South denied the right of the North, acting through the Central Government, to interfere with its "peculiar institution"; and even those who deplored the existence of slavery felt themselves none the less bound to assert and defend the right of their respective States to manage their own affairs.[9] It was a conflict as old as the Revolution—and even, in its germs, of still older date—between centripetal and centrifugal forces, between national and local patriotism. The makers of the Constitution had tried to hold the scales justly, but in their natural jealousy of a strong central power, they had allowed the balance to deflect unduly on the side of local independence. The North, the national majority, felt, obscurely and reluctantly, that a revision of the Constitution in the matter of slavery was essential to the national welfare. The South maintained that the States were antecedent and superior to the Nation, and said, " If your Nation, in virtue of its mere majority vote, insists on encroaching on State rights which we formally reserved as a condition of entering the Nation, why then, we prefer to withdraw from this Nation and set up a nation of our own, in which the true principles of the Constitution shall be preserved." Thereupon the North retorted, " We deny your right to withdraw," and the battle was joined.

The North said," You have no right to withdraw," but it meant, I think, something rather different. It

> [9] " Submission to any encroachment," says Professor Gilder-sleeve, " the least as well as the greatest, on the rights of a State, means slavery"; this remark occurring early in an article of twenty-five columns, in which *negro* slavery is not so much as mentioned until the twenty-first column.

See Postscript to this article.

threw overboard the question of abstract, formal, technical right, and fought primarily, no doubt, for a humanitarian ideal, but fundamentally to enforce its instinct of the highest political expediency. The right interpretation of a state-paper, however venerable, would not have been a question worthy of such terrible arbitrament. Even the emancipation of the negro, had that been the sole object of the contest, would have been too dearly paid for in blood and tears. The question at issue was really this: What is the ideal political unit ? The largest possible ? or the smallest convenient ? What mattered abstract argument as to the right to secede ? Once grant the *power* to secede, once suffer the precedent to be established, and the greatest democracy the world had ever seen was bound to break up, not only into two, but ultimately into many petty republics, wrangling and jangling like those of Spanish America. To this negation of a great ideal the North refused its consent. National patriotism had outgrown local patriotism. It had become to all intents and purposes a fiction that the Federal Government derived its powers from the States.

Thirteen of them, indeed, had sanctioned the Federal Government, but the Federal Government had sanctioned and admitted to the Union twenty-one more. In these the sentiment of priority to the Union could not exist, while State Sovereignty was a doctrine limited by considerations of expediency, rather than a patriotic dogma. Immigration, and westward migration from the north-eastern States, had produced a race of men and women whose patriotism was divorced, so to speak, from any given patch of soil, but was wedded to the all-embracing idea of the United States, with the emphasis on the epithet. They thought of themselves first of all as American citizens, and only in the second place as citizens of this State or of that. This habit or instinct is still incomprehensible, and almost contemptible, to the Southerner of the older generation; but the Time-Spirit was clearly on its side.

Thus, then, I interpret the fundamental feeling which impelled the North to take up arms : " Better one stout tussle for the idea of Unity than a facile acquiescence in the idea of Multiplicity, with all its sequels of instability, distrust, rivalry, and rancour. Better for our children, if not for us, one great expenditure of blood and gold than never-ending ' threats and rumours of war, commercial conflicts, political complications, frontiers to be safeguarded, bureaucracies to be financed." Of course I do not put this forward as a new interpretation of the question at issue. It is old and it is obvious. But though the national significance of the struggle has long been recognised, I am not sure that its international, its world-historic, significance has been sufficiently dwelt upon. We Europeans have been apt to think that, because the theatre of conflict was so distant, we had only a spectacular, or at most an abstract-humanitarian, interest in it. There could not be a greater mistake. The whole world, I believe, will one day come to hold Vicksburg and Gettysburg names of larger historic import than Waterloo or Sedan.

IV

The iconoclast of to-day is full of scorn for patriotism, which he holds the most retrograde of emotions. He may as usefully declaim against friendship, comradeship, the love of man for woman or of mother for child. The lowest savage regards himself, and cannot but regard himself, as a member of some sort of political aggregation. This feeling is one of the primal instincts of humanity, and as such one of the permanent' data of the problem of the future. It is folly to 'denounce or seek to eradicate it. The wise course is to give it large and noble instead of petty and parochial concepts to which to attach itself. Rightly esteemed and rightly directed, patriotism is not a retrograde emotion, but one of the indispensable conditions of progress.

" Nothing is," says Hamlet, " but thinking makes it so." It is not oceans, straits, rivers, or mountain-barriers that constitute a Nation, but the idea in the minds of the people composing it. Now, the largest political idea that ever entered the mind—not of a man—not of a governing class—but of a people, is the idea of the United States of America. The " Pax Romana" was a great idea in its day, but it was imposed from without, and by military methods, upon a number of subject peoples, who did not realise and intelligently co-operate in it, but merely submitted to it. It has its modern analogue in the " Pax Britannica " of India. The idea of the United States, on the other hand, gives what may be called psychological unity to one of the largest political aggregates, both in territory and population, ever known to history. In the modern world there are only two political aggregates in any wise comparable to it: the British Empire, whereof the idea is not as yet quite clearly formulated; and the Russian Empire, whereof the idea, in so far as it belongs to the people at all, is a blind and slavish superstition. Holy Russia is a formidable idea, Greater Britain is a picturesque and pregnant idea; but the United States is a self-conscious, clearly defined and heroically vindicated idea, in whose further vindication the whole world is concerned.

It is only an experiment, say some—an experiment which, thirty years ago, trembled on the brink of disastrous failure, and which may yet have even greater perils to encounter. This is true in a sense, but not the essential truth. Let us substitute for " experiment" another word which means the same thing—with a difference. The United States of America, let us say, is a rehearsal for the United States of Europe, nay, of the world. It is the very difficulties over which the croakers shake their heads that make the experiment interesting, momentous. The United States is a veritable microcosm: it presents in little all the elements which go to make up a world, and which have hitherto kept the world, almost unintermittently, in a state of battle and bloodshed. There are wide differences of climate and of geo-. graphical conditions in the United States, with the resulting conflict of material interest between different regions of the country. There are differences of race and even of language to be overcome, extremes of wealth and poverty to be dealt with. As though to make sure that no factor in the problem of civilisation should be omitted, the men of last century were at pains to saddle their descendants with the burden of the negro—a race incapable of assimilation and yet tenacious of life. In brief, a thousand difficulties and temptations to dissension beset the giant Republic: in so far as it overcomes them, and carries on its development by peaceful methods, it presents a unique and invaluable object-lesson to the world. The idea of unity, annealed in the furnace of the Civil War, has as yet been stronger than all the forces of disintegration; and there is no reason to doubt that it will continue to be so. When France falls out with Germany, or Russia with Turkey, there is nothing save a purely material counting of the cost to hinder them from flying at each other's throats. The abstract humanitarianism of a few individuals is as a feather on the torrent. Such sentiment as comes into play is all on the side of bloodshed. It takes very little to make a Frenchman and a German feel that they are in a state of war by nature, and that peace between them is an artificial and necessarily unstable condition. But in America, should two States or two groups of States fall out, there is a strong, and we may hope unconquerable, sentiment of unity to be overcome before the dissentients even reach the point of counting the material cost of war. Men feel that they are in a state of peace by nature, and that war between them, instead of being a hereditary and almost consecrated habit, would be a monstrous and almost unthinkable crime. The National Government, as established by the Constitution, is in fact a permanent court of abitration between the States; and the common-sense of all may be trusted to "hold a fractious State in awe." "Did not people say and think the same thing in 1859," it may be asked, " on the eve of the greatest Civil War in history ? " Possibly; but that war was precisely what was needed to ratify the Union, and lift it out of the experimental stage. "Blut ist ein ganz besondrer Saft," and it is sometimes necessary that other pacts than those of hell should be written in blood, before the world recognises their full validity. Heaven forbid that the Deed of Union of the United States should require a second time to be retraced in red!

But it is an illusion, though a salutary one, that civil war is any more barbarous than international war. What the world wants is the realisation that every war is a civil war, a war between brothers, justifiable only for the repression of some cruelty more cruel than war itself, some barbarism more barbarous. Towards this realisation the United States is leading the way, by showing that, under the conditions of modern life, an effective sense of brotherhood, a resolute loyalty to a unifying idea, may be maintained throughout a practically unlimited extent of territory.

But, while enumerating the difficulties which the Republic has to overcome, I have said nothing of the one great advantage it enjoys—a common, or at any rate a dominant, language. The diversity of tongues which prevails in Europe is doubtless one of the chief hindrances to that " Federation of the World" of which the poet dreamed. But if the many tongues of Europe retard its fusion into what I have called a political aggregate, there exists in the world a political aggregate larger in extent than either Europe or the United States, which possesses, like the United States, the advantage of one dominant language. I mean, of course, the British Empire; and surely it is, on the face of it, a fact of good augury for the world that the dominant language of these two vast aggregations of democracies should happen to be one and the same. The hopes—and perhaps, too, some apprehensions— arising from this unity of speech will form the subject of another article.

POSTSCRIPT.—My representation of the South as the conservative and the North as the innovating party is the only point in this article to which (so far as I know) serious objection has been made. A very able and courteous critic—Mr. Norman Hapgood—writes to me as follows: " I think the history of the Kansas-Nebraska trouble, in which the preliminary conflict centred, the speeches of the time, North and South, the party platforms, all proved that the North said, ' Slavery shall keep its rights and have no further extension/ while the South said, 'It shall go into any newly acquired territory it chooses.' In 1860 the slave interest was more protected and extended by law than ever before in the history of the country. It had simply made a new claim which the North could not allow. The abolitionists were few; the Northerners who said that slavery should not be ***extended*** were many...I don't believe there is an American historian of standing who does not say that the propositions of the South, on which the North took issue in 1861, were these: (1) Slavery shall go into all territory hereafter acquired; (2) We will secede if this is not allowed."

It was inevitable that this protest should be raised, since, in the limited space at my command, I had imperfectly expressed my meaning. My reply to Mr. Hapgood puts it, I hope, more clearly. It ran as follows: "What I was trying to do was not so much to summarise conscious motives as to present my own interpretation (right or wrong) of the sub-conscious, the unconscious forces that were at work. I go behind the declarations of Northern statesmen, and what, I have no doubt, was the sincere sentiment of the majority in the North, against interference with slavery in the existing slave States. I have tried to allow to this sentiment what weight it deserves, in saying that the North ' *obscurely and re-luctantly* felt a revision of the Constitution essential to the national welfare.' But my view is that whatever they said, and whatever, on the surface of their minds, they thought, the people of the North knew, even if they denied it to themselves, that chattel slavery was impossible in the modern world; and furthermore that the people of the South were justified in that instinct which told them that the institution, fatally menaced, was to be saved only by secession. The kernel of the matter, to my thinking, lay in the fugitive slave question. The provision of the Constitution for the return of fugitive slaves, though it may seem a matter of detail, was, I think, in reality the keystone of the arch. Make it inoperative, and the institution was doomed. Now many of the Northern States, by ' personal liberty laws' and the like, had long been picking at that keystone. Whatever were the professions of politicians and people as to non-interference, they shrank from the logical corollary, which would have been the sincere, whole-hearted and cheerful carrying out of Article IV., Section 2, Paragraph 3 of the Constitution. They were wen, I think, logically bound to accept loyally the Dred Scott decision, which was absolutely constitutional. To protest against it, to seek to evade it, was to insist on a revision of the Constitution. But it was inconceivable that a civilised community, not blinded by local Southern prejudice, could loyally accept the Dred Scott decision, or could cheerfully assist the Southern slaveholder to capture and carry off from their own hearthstones, as it were, his runaway chattel. Therefore, the position and the pro-testations of the North were mutually contradictory. It was a case of trying to run with the hare and hunt with the hounds; and the North was bound to the hare by fundamental con-siderations of humanity and self-interest, to the hounds only by a compact accepted at a time when its consequences could not possibly be foreseen. I do not doubt that the North, on the surface of its will, sincerely desired to keep this compact; but the South, with an instinct which was really that of self-preservation, looked, as I am trying to look, beneath the conscious surface to the unconscious sweep of current. It is not with reference to the struggle for Western expansion that I call the South the conservative and constitutional party. There, as it seems to me, the question was entirely an open one, the power of Congress over territories being undefined in the Constitution; and no doubt the South, in the course of the struggle, often took up violent and extravagant positions. My argument is that the attitude of the North, whatever its protestations, virtually threatened the institution of slavery in the old slave States, and that therefore the South had virtual, if not formal, justification for holding the constitutional compact broken."

THE REPUBLIC AND THE EMPIRE

I

THOUGH one of the main objects which I proposed to myself in visiting America was to take note of American feeling towards England as affected by the Spanish War, I soon found that, so far as the gathering of information by way of question and answer was concerned, I might almost as well have stayed at home. A curious diffidence beset me from the first. I shrank from recognising that there was any question as to the good feeling between the two countries, and still more from seeming to appeal to a non-existent or a grudging sense of kinship. It seemed to me tactless and absurd for an Englishman to lay any stress on the war as affecting the relations between the two peoples. What had England done? Nothing that had cost her a cent or a drop of blood. The British people had sympathised with the United States in a war which it felt to be, in the last analysis, a part of the necessary policework of the world ; it had applauded in American soldiers and sailors the qualities it was accustomed to admire in its own fighting men ; and the British Government, giving ready effect to the instinct of the people, had, at a critical moment, secured a fair field for the United States, and broken up what might have been an embarrassing, though scarcely a very formidable, anti-American intrigue on the part of the Continental Powers. What was there in all this to make any merit of? Nothing whatever. It was the simplest matter in the world—we had merely felt and done what came natural to us. The really significant fact was that any one in America should have been surprised at our attitude, or should have regarded it as more friendly than they had every right and reason to expect. In short, I felt an irrational but I hope not unnatural disinclination to recognise as matter for question and remark a state of feeling which, as it seemed to me, ought to " go without saying."

Above all was I careful to avoid the word " Anglo-Saxon." I heard it and read it with satisfaction: I uttered it, never. It is for the American to claim his Anglo-Saxon birthright, if he feels so disposed; it is not for the Briton to thrust it upon him. To cheapen it, to send it a-begging, were to do it a grievous wrong. Besides, the term " Anglo-Saxon " is inaccurate, and, so to speak, provisional. Rightly understood, it covers a great idea; but if one chooses to take it in a strict ethnological sense, it lends itself to caricature. The truth is, it has no strict ethnological sense—it may rather be called an ethnological countersense, no less in England than in America. It represents an historical and political, not an ethnological, concept. The Anglo-Saxon was already an infinitely composite personage—Saxon, Scandinavian, Gaul, and Kelt—before he set foot in America; and America merely proves her deep-rooted Anglo-Saxonism in accepting and absorbing all sorts of alien and semi-alien race-elements. But when we have to go so far behind the face-value of a word to bring it into consonance with obvious facts, it is safest to use that word sparingly.

In brief, I did not wear my Anglo-Saxon heart on my sleeve, or go about inviting expressions of gratitude to England for having, like Mr. Gilbert's House of Lords,

Done nothing in particular,

And done it very well.

Yet evidences of a new tone of feeling towards England met me on every hand, both in the news-papers and in conversation. The subject which I shrank from introducing was frequently introduced by my American acquaintances. It was evident that the change of feeling, though far from universal, was real and widespread. Americans who had recently returned to their native land, after passing some years abroad, assured me that they were keenly conscious of it. Many of my acquaintances were opposed to the policy which brought about the Spanish War, and declared the better mutual understanding between England and America to be its one good result. Others adopted the view to which Mr. Kipling had given such far-echoing expression, and frankly rejoiced in the sympathy with which England regarded America's determination to " take up the white man's burden." In the Kipling craze as a whole, after making all deductions, I could not but see a symptom of real significance. It was partly a mere literary fashion, partly a result of personal and accidental circumstances; but it also arose in no small degree from a novel sense of kinship with the men, and participation in the ideals, celebrated by the poet of British Imperialism.

The change, moreover, extended beyond the book-reading class, wide as that is in America. It was to be noted even in the untravelled and unlettered American, the man whose spiritual horizon is bounded by his Sunday newspaper, the man in the street and on the farm. The events of the past year had taught him—and he rubbed his eyes at the realisation—that England was not an "effete monarchy," evilly disposed towards a Republic as such,[10] and dully resentful of bygone humiliations by land and sea, but a brotherly-minded people, remembering little (perhaps *too* little) of those " old, unhappy, far-off things," willing to be as helpful as the rules of neutrality permitted, and eager to applaud the achievements of American arms.

[10] *See* Postscript to this article.

Millions of people who had hitherto felt no touch of racial sympathy, and had been conscious only of a vague historic antipathy, learned with surprise that England was in no sense their natural enemy, but rather, among all the nations of Europe, their natural friend. Anglophobes, no doubt, were still to be found in plenty; but they could no longer reckon on the instant popular response which, a few years ago, would almost certainly have attended any movement of hostility towards England. An American publicist, who has perhaps unequalled opportunities for keeping his finger on the pulse of national feeling, said to me, " It is only three or four years since I heard a Federal judge express an earnest desire for war with England, as a means of consolidating the North and South in a great common enthusiasm. Of course this was pernicious talk at any time," he added; " but it would then have found an echo which it certainly would not find today."

This puts the international situation in a nutshell, so far as to-day is concerned. But what about tomorrow ?

II

When people spoke to me of the sudden veering of popular sympathy from France and Russia, and towards England, I could not help asking, now and again, " When is the reaction coming ? " " " There is no reaction coming,"1 was told with some confidence. For my own part, I hope and believe that a permanent advance had been made, and that any reaction that may set in will be trifling and temporary. But to ensure this result there is still the most urgent need for the exercise of wisdom and moderation on both sides. The misunderstandings of more than a century are not to be wiped out in two or three months of popular excitement. What we have arrived at is not a complete mutual understanding, but merely the attitude of mind which may, in course of time, render such an understanding possible. That, to be sure, is half the battle; but the longer and more tedious half is before us.

The Englishman who visits America for pleasure, and enjoys the inexhaustible hospitality of New York, Boston, and Washington, must be careful not to imagine that he gets really in touch with the senti-ment of the American nation. His circle of acquaintance is almost certain to be composed mainly of people whom he, or friends of his, have met in Europe, people of more or less clearly remembered British descent, who know England well, have many English friends and possibly relatives, and are conscious of a distinct sentimental attachment to " the Old Country." They are almost without exception people of culture, as well read as he himself in the English classics, ancient and modern. They show their Americanism not in that they love English literature less, but that very probably they love French literature more, than he does. Further, they are an exceedingly polite people, and, sensitive them-selves on points of national honour, they instinctively keep in the background all topics on which a too free interchange of opinions might be apt to wound the susceptibilities of their guest. Thus he loses entirely his sense of being in a foreign country, because he moves among people most of whom have an affection for England almost as deep as his own, while all are courteous enough to respect his prejudices. This class is large in actual numbers, no doubt, but in proportion to the whole American people it is infinitesimal, and would be a mere featherweight in the scale at any moment of crisis. Its voice is clearly audible in literature and even in journalism, but at the polls it would be as a whisper to the thunder of Niagara. The traveller who has " had a good time " in literary, artistic, university circles in the Eastern cities, has not felt the pulse of America, but has merely touched the fringe of the fringe of her garment.

We deceive ourselves if we imagine that there is, or at any rate that there was until recently, the slightest sentimental attachment to England in the heart of the American people at large. Among the " hyphenated Americans," as they are called—Irish-Americans, German-Americans, and so forth — it would be folly to look for any such feeling.[11] The

[11] A very distinguished American authority writes to me as follows with regard to this passage: "I hardly think you lay enough weight upon the fact that in two or three generations the

conciliation of America will never be complete until we have achieved the conciliation of Ireland. It is evident, indeed, from many symptoms, that Irish-American hostility to England is declining, if not in rancour, at any rate in influence. Still, a popular New York paper, on St. Patrick's Day, thinks it worth while to propitiate " The Powerful Race of Ireland " by a leader under that heading, and to this effect:

" The Irish race is famous as producing the best fighters and poets among men, and the most beautiful and most virtuous of women.

" Such a reputation should suffice for any nation.

" And note that Ireland still is and always will be a NATION. There is no Anglomania in that fair land, no yearning for reciprocity for the sake of a few dollars, no drinking of the Queen's health first...

great bulk of the descendants of the immigrants of non-English origin become absolutely indistinguishable from other Americans, and share their feelings. This is markedly so with the Scandinavians, and most of the Germans of the second, and all the Germans of the third, generation, who practically all, during 1898, felt toward Germany and England just exactly as other Americans didTwice recently I have addressed huge meetings of eight or ten thousand people, each drawn, as regards the enormous majority, from exactly that class which you pointed out as standing between the two extremes. In each case the men who introduced me dwelt upon the increased good feeling between the English-speaking peoples, and very complimentary allusion to England was received with great rapplause." At the same time my correspondent adds: " Your, division of the American sentiment into three classes is exactly right; also your sense of the relative importance of these there classes."

" Noble patriots like John Dillon and Willam O'Brien fight for them in the House of Commons, and they are good fighters everywhere, from the glass-covered room in Westminster Abbey (!) to the prize-ring, where a Sullivan, of pure Irish b ood, forbids any man to stand three rounds before him.

" The English whipped the Irish at the battle of the Boyne— true. But the English on that occasion had the good luck to be led by a Dutchman, and the Irish— sorra the day—had an English King for a leader. The English King was running fast while the Irish were still fighting the Dutchman.

" Wellington, of Irish blood, beat Napoleon; Sheridan, of Irish blood, fought here most delightfully.

"Here's to the Irish!"

This spirited performance no doubt represents fairly enough the political philosophy of the thousands composing the league-long procession which filed stolidly up Fifth Avenue on the day of its appearance.

But even among unhyphenated Americans— Americans pure and simple—the tendency to regard England as a hereditary foe, though sensibly weakened by recent events, remains very strong. A good example of this frame of mind and habit of speech is afforded by the following passage from an address delivered by Judge Van Wyck at the Democratic Club's Jefferson Dinner in New York on April 13 last. Referring to England, the speaker said :

" Let us be influenced by the natural as well as the fixed policy of that nation toward us for a century and a half, rather than by their profuse expressions of friendship during the Spanish War. England's policy has been one of sharp rivalry and competition with America; it impelled the Revolution of 1776, fought for business as well as political independence; brought on the war of 1812, waged against the insolent claim of England for the right to search our ships of commerce while riding the highways of the ocean; caused her to contest every inch of our northern boundary line from ocean to ocean; made her encourage our family troubles from 1860 to 1865, for which she was compelled to pay us millions and admit her wrong; and actuated her, in violation of the Monroe doctrine, to attempt an unwarrantable encroachment on the territory of Venezuela, until ordered by the American Government to halt."

Apart from the obvious begging of the question with reference to Venezuela, there is nothing in this invective that has not some historical foundation. It is the studiously hostile turn of the phraseology that renders the speech significant. Everything— even the honourable amends made for the *Alabama* blunder—is twisted to England's reproach. She is " compelled " to do this, and " ordered " to do that. There is here no hint of good feeling, no trace of international amenity, but sheer undisguised hatred and desire to make the worst of things. And this address, be it noted, was the speech of the evening at a huge and representative gathering of the dominant party in New York municipal politics.

I need scarcely adduce further evidence of the fact that Anglophobia is still a power in the land, if not the power it once was. But active and aggressive Anglophobia is, I think, a less important factor in the situation than the sheer indifference to England, with a latent bias towards hostility, which is so widespread in America. To the English observer, this indifference is far more disconcerting than hatred. The average Briton, one may say with confidence, is not indifferent towards America. He may be very ignorant about it, very much prejudiced against certain American habits and institutions, very thoughtless and tactless in expressing his prejudices ; but the United States is not, to him, a foreign country like any other, on the same plane with France, Germany, or Russia. But that is precisely what England is to millions of Americans—a foreign country like any other. We see this even in many travelling Americans; much more is it to be noted in multitudes who stay at home. Many Americans seem curiously indifferent even to the comfort of being able to speak their own language in England; probably because they have less false shame than the average Englishman in adventuring among the pitfalls of a foreign tongue. They—this particular class of travellers, I mean — land in England without emotion, visit its shrines without sentiment, and pass on to France and Italy with no other feeling than one of relief in escaping from the London fog. These travellers, however, are but single spies sent forth by vast battalions who never cross the ocean. To them England is a mere name, and the name, moreover, of their fathers' one enemy in war, their own chief rival in trade. They have no points of contact with England, such as almost every Englishman has with America. We make use every day of American inventions and American " notions" : English inventions and " notions," if they make their way to America at all, are not recognised as English. There are few Britishers, high or low, that have not friends or relatives settled in America, or have not formed pleasant acquaintanceships with Americans on this side. But there are innumerable families in America who, even if they be of British descent, have lost all vital recollection of the fact; who (as the tide of emigration has not yet turned eastwards) have no friends or relatives settled in England; and who, in their American homes, are far more apt to come in contact with men of almost every other nationality than with Englishmen. " But surely English literature," it may be said, " brings England home even to people of this class, and differentiates her from France or Germany." In a measure, doubtless; but I think it will be found that the lower strata of the reading public (not in America alone, of course) are strangely insensitive to local colour. To people of culture, the bond of literature is a very strong one; but the class of which I am speaking is not composed of people of culture. They read, it is true, and often greedily; but generally, I think, without knowing or greatly caring whether a book is English or American, and at all events with no such clear perception of the distinctive qualities of English work as could beget in them any imaginative realisation of, or affection for, England. Let us make no mistake—in the broad mass of the American people no such affection exists. They are simply indifferent to England, with, as I have said, a latent bias towards hostility.

Thus the scale of American feeling towards England, while its gradations are of course infinite, may be divided into three main sections. At one end of the scale we have the cultured and travelled classes, especially in the Eastern States, conscious for the most part of British descent, alive to the historical relationship between the two countries, valuing highly their birthright in the treasures of English literature, knowing, and (not uncritically) understanding England and her people, and clinging to a kinship of which, taking one thing with another, they have no reason to be ashamed. This class is intellectually influential, but its direct weight in politics is small. It is, with shining exceptions, a " mugwump " class. At the other end of the scale we have the hyphenated Americans, who have imported or inherited European rancours against England, and those unhyphenated Americans whose hatred of England is partly a mere plank in a political platform, designed to accommodate her hyphenated foemen, partly a result of instinctive and traditional chauvinism, reinforced by a (in every sense) partial view of Anglo-American history. Finally, between these two extremes, we have the great mass of the American people, who neither love nor hate England, any more than they love or hate (say) Italy or Japan, but whose indifference would, until recently, have been much more easily deflected on the side of hatred than of love. The effect of the Spanish War has been in some measure to alter this bias, and to differentiate England, to her advantage, from the other nations of Europe.

III

It is commonly alleged that the anti-English virulence of the ordinary school history of the United States is mainly responsible for this bias towards hostility in the mind of the average American. Mr. Goldwin Smith, a high authority, has contested this theory; and I must admit that, after a good deal of inquiry, I have been unable to find the American school historians guilty of any very serious injustices to England. Some quite modern histories which I have looked into (yet written before the Spanish War) seem to me excellently and most impartially. done. The older histories are not well written: they are apt to be sensational and chauvinistic in tone, and to encourage a somewhat cheap and blusterous order of patriotism ; but that they commonly malign character or misrepresent events I cannot discover. They are perhaps a little too much inclined to make " insolent" the inseparable epithet of the British soldier; but there is no reason to doubt that in many cases it was amply merited. I have not come across the history in which Mr. G. W. Steevens discovered the following passages:

" The eyes of the soldiers glared upon the people like hungry bloodhounds. The captain waved his sword. The red-coats pointed their guns at the crowd. In a moment the flash of their muskets lighted up the street, and eleven New England men fell bleeding upon the snowBlood was streaming upon the snow; and though that purple stain melted away in the next day's sun, it was never forgotten nor forgiven by the people A battle took place between a large force of Tories and Indians and a hastily organised force of patriotic Americans. The Americans were defeated with horrible slaughter, and many of those who were made prisoners were put to death by fiendish torture. More than six thousand American sailors had been seized by British warships and pressed into the hated service of a hated nation."

These passages are certainly not judicial or even judicious in tone; but I fancy that the book or books from which Mr. Steevens culled them must be quite anti-quated. In books at present on the educational market I find nothing so lurid. What I do find in some is a failure to distinguish between the king's share and the British people's share in the policy which brought about and carried on the Revolutionary War. For instance, in Barnes's *Primary History of the United States* (undated, but brought down to the end of the Spanish War) we read :

' *The English people* after a time became jealous of the prosperity of the colo-nists, and began to devise plans by which to grasp for themselves a share of the wealth that was thus rolling inIndeed, *the English people* acted from the first as if the colonies existed only for the purpose of helping them to make money."

George III. and his Ministers are not so much as mentioned, and the impression conveyed to the ingenuous student is that the whole English nation was consciously and deliberately banded together for purposes of sheer brigandage. The same his-tory is delightfully chauvinistic in its account of the Colonial Wars. The British officers are all bunglers and poltroons; if disasters are averted or victories won, it is entirely by the courage and conduct of the colonists:

" When Johnson reached the head of Lake George he met the French, and a fierce battle was fought. Success seemed at first to be altogether with the French; but after a while Johnson was slightly wounded, when General Lyman, a brave co-lonial officer, took command, and beat the French terribly…Abercrombie's defeat was the last of the English disasters. The colonists now had arms enough, and were allowed to fight in their own way, and a series of brilliant victories followed By the energy, courage, and patriotism of her colonies, England had now acquired a splendid empire in the New World. And while she reaped all the glory of the war and its fruits, it was the hardy colonists who had, throughout, borne the brunt of the conflict."

The child who learns his history from Mr. Barnes may not hate England, but will certainly despise her.

Text-books of this type, however, are already obsolescent. A committee of the New England History Teachers' Association published in the ***Educational Review*** for December 1898 a careful survey of no fewer than nineteen school histories of the United States, and summed up the results as follows :

" In discussing the causes of the Revolution, text-book writers have sounded pretty much the whole scale of motives. England has been pictured, on the one hand, as an arbitrary oppressor, and, on the other, as the helpless victim of political environment. Under the influence of deeper study and a keener sense of justice, however, the element of bitterness, which so often entered into the discussion of this subject, has largely disappeared ; and while the treatment of the Revolution in the text-books still leaves much to be desired, it is now seldom dogmatic and unsympathetic."

The fact remains, however, that we have still to live down our wars with the United States, in which there was much that was galling to the just pride of the American people, and much, too, that was perhaps over-stimulating to their self-esteem. There is no doubt, on the one hand, that we were inclined to adopt a supercilious and contemptuous attitude towards the "rebel colonists" of 1775, the new-made nation of 1815; no doubt, on the other hand, that they made a splendid fight against us, and taught our superciliousness a salutary lesson. They feel to this day the humiliation of having been despised, and the exultation of having put their despisers to shame. These wars, which were, until 1861, almost the whole military history of the United States, were but episodes in our history, and one of them a trifling episode. Therefore, while the average Englishman has not studied them sufficiently to realise how much he ought to deplore them, the average American has been taught to dwell upon them as the glorious struggles in which his nation won its spurs. To the juvenile imagination, battles are always the oases in the desert of history, and the schoolboy never fails to take sides fiercely and uncompromisingly, exaggerating, with the histrionic instinct of youth, his enthusiasm and his hatreds. Thus the insolent Britisher became the Turk's-head or Guy Fawkes, so to speak, of the American boy, the butt of his bellicose humours; and a habit of mind contracted in boyhood is not always to be eradicated by the sober reflection of manhood, even in minds capable of sober reflection. The Civil War, be it noted, did not depose the insolent Britisher from his bad eminence in the schoolboy imagination. The Confederates were, after all, Americans, though misguided Americans; and the fostering, the brooding upon, intestine rancours was felt by teachers and pupils alike to be impossible. But there is in the juvenile mind at any given moment a certain amount of abstract combativeness, let us call it, which must find an outlet somewhere. Hatred is a natural function of the human mind, just as much as love; and the healthy boy instinctively exercises it under the guise of patriotism, without clearly distinguishing the element of sheer play and pose in his transports. England's attitude during the Civil War certainly did nothing to endear her either to the writers or the readers of school histories; and she remained after that struggle, as she had been before, the one great historical adversary on whom the abstract combativeness of young America could expend itself. How strong this tendency is, or has been, in the American school, may be judged from the following anecdote. A boy of unmixed English parentage, whose father and mother had settled in America, was educated at the public school of his district. On the day when Mr. Cleveland's Venezuela message was given to the world, he came home from school radiant, and shouted to his parents : " Hurrah 1 We're going to war with England 1 We've whipped you twice before, and we're going to do it again." It is clear that at this academy Anglomania formed no part of the curriculum; and who can doubt that in myriads of cases these schoolboy animosities subsist throughout life, either active or dormant and easily awakened ?

Let us admit without shrinking that the history of the United States cannot be truthfully written in such a way as to ingratiate Great Britain with the youth of America. There have been painful episodes between the two nations, in which England has, on the whole, acted stupidly, or arrogantly, or both. Nor can we shift the whole blame upon George III. or his Ministers. They were responsible for the actual Revolution; but after the Revolution, down even to the time of the Civil War inclusive, the English people, though guiltless in the main of active hostility to America, cannot be acquitted of ignorance and indifference. It is not in the least to be desired that American history should be written with a pro-English bias, and, as

I have said, I do not find the anti-English bias, even in inferior text-books, so excessive as it is sometimes represented to be. The anti-English sentiment of American schools is, as it seems to me, an inevitable phenomenon of juvenile psychology, under the given conditions; and it is the alteration in the actual conditions wrought by recent events, rather than any marked change in the tone of the text-books, that may, I think, be trusted to soothe the schoolboy's savage breast. England has now done what she had never done before: shown herself conspicuously friendly to the United States; and another European country has given occasion for spirit-stirring manifestations of American prowess. Thus England is deposed for the time, and we may trust for ever, from her position as the one traditional arch-enemy.

But though the errors of commission in American history-books have been exaggerated, I cannot but think that a common error of omission is worthy of remark and correction. They begin American history too late—with the discovery of America— and they do not awaken, as they might, the just pride of race in the " unhyphenated " American boy. Long before Columbus set sail from Palos, American history was a-making in the shire-moots of Saxon England, at Hastings, and Runnymead, and Ban-nockburn. In all the mediaeval achievements of England, in peace and war—in her cathedrals, her castles, her universities, in Cressy, Poictiers, and Agincourt—Americans may without paradox claim their ancestral part. Why should the sons of the English who emigrated leave to the sons of those who stayed at home the undivided credit of having sent to the right-about the Invincible Armada? Nay, it is only the very oldest American families that can disclaim all complicity in having, as Lord Auchinleck put it, " garred kings ken that they had a lith in their necks." Of course I do not mean that the American schoolboy should be taken in detail through British history down to the seventeenth century before, so to speak, he crosses the Atlantic. But I do suggest that he would be none the worse American for being encouraged to set a due value on his rightful share in the achievements of earlier ancestors than those who fought at Trenton or sailed with Decatur. Let him realise his birthright in the glories of Britain, and he will perhaps come to take a more magnanimous view of her errors and disasters.

IV

Britain has been too forgetful of the past, America, perhaps, too mindful; and in the everyday relations of life Britain has often been tactless and unsympathetic, America suspicious and supersensitive. There is every prospect, I think, that such errors will become, in the future, rarer and ever rarer; and it behoves us, on our side, to be careful in guarding against them. We have not hitherto sufficiently respected America—that is the whole story. We have taken no pains to know and understand her. We have too often regarded her with a careless and supercilious good feeling, which she has not unnaturally mistaken for ill feeling, and repaid in kind. The events of the past year seem to have brought the two countries almost physically closer to each other, and to have made them more real, more clearly visible, each to each. America has won the respectful consideration of even the most thoughtless and insular among us. She has come home to us, so to speak, as a vast and vital factor in the problem of the future. Superciliousness towards her is a mere anachronism.

Many Englishmen, however, are still guilty of a thoughtless captiousness towards America, which is none the less galling because it manifests itself in the most trifling matters. A friend of my own returned a few years ago from a short tour in the United States, declaring that he heartily disliked the country, and would never go back again. Inquiry as to the grounds of his dissatisfaction elicited no more definite or damning charge than that " they " (a collective pronoun presumed to cover the whole American people) hung up his trousers instead of folding them—or *vice versa,* for I am heathen enough not to remember which is the orthodox process. Doubtless he had other, and possibly weightier, causes of complaint; but this was the head and front of America's offending. Another Englishman of education and position, being asked why he had never crossed the Atlantic, gravely replied that he could not endure to travel in a country where you had to black your own boots! Such instances of ignorance and pettiness may seem absurdly trivial, but they are quite sufficient to act as grits in the machinery of social intercourse. Americans are very fond of citing as an example of English manners the legend of a great lady who, at an American breakfast, saw her husband declining a dish which was offered to him, and called across the table, " Take some, my dear—it isn't half as nasty as it looks." Three different people have vouched to me for the truth of this anecdote, each naming the heroine, and each giving her a different name. True or false, it is held in America to be typical; and it would scarcely be so popular as it is unless people had suffered a good deal from the tactlessness which it exemplifies. The same vice, in a more insidious form, appears in a remark made to me the other day by an Englishman of very high intelligence, who had just returned from a long tour in America, and was, in the main, far from unsympathetic. "What I felt," he said, " was the suburbanism of everything. It was all Claphamor Camberwell on a gigantic scale." Some justice of observation may possibly have lain behind this remark, though I certainly failed to recognise it. But in the form of its expression it exemplified that illusion of metropolitanism which is to my mind the veriest cockneyism in disguise, and which cannot but strike Americans as either ridiculous or offensive.

Englishmen who, as individuals, wish to promote and not impede an international understanding, will do well to take some little thought to avoid wounding, even in trifles, the just and inevitable suscepti-bilities of their American acquaintances. Our own national self-esteem is cased in oak and triple brass,[12] and we are apt to regard American sensitiveness as a ridiculous foible. It is nothing of the sort: it is a psychological necessity, deep-rooted in history and social conditions.

Again, there are certain misunderstandings which Englishmen, not as individual human beings but as citizens of the British Empire, ought carefully to guard against. Let us beware of speaking or thinking as though friendship for England involved on the part of America any acceptance of English political ideas or imitation of English methods. In especial, let us carefully guard against the idea that an Anglo-American understanding, however cordial, implies the adoption of an " expansionist " policy by the United States, or must necessarily strengthen the hands of the " expansionist" party. If America

[12] I do not mean that we are callous to American criticism, or always take it in good part when it comes home to us. I think with shame, for example, of the stupid insolence with which certain English journalists used for years to treat Mr. W. D. Howells, merely because he had expressed certain literary judgments from which they dissented. What I do mean, and believe to be true, is that we are *habitually unconscious* of American criticism, while Americans may rather be said to be *habitually over-conscious* that the eyes of England and of the world are on them. The existence of this habit of mind seems to me no less evident than the fact that it is rapidly correcting itself. chooses to " take up the white man's burden 'in the Kiplingesque sense, it would ill become England to object; but her doing so is by no means a condition of England's sympathy. It might seem, indeed, that she had plenty of " white man's burden " to shoulder within her own continental boundaries; but that is a matter which she is entirely competent to determine for herself.

Most of all must we beware of anything that can encourage an impression, already too prevalent in America, that we find the "white man's burden" too heavy for us, and are anxious to share it with the United States. This suspicion is very generally felt and very openly expressed. Take, for instance, this paragraph from an editorial in one of the leading Chicago papers:

" It would be a strange thing to see Continental Europe take up arms against Great Britain alone. . . . That it is a very reasonable possibility, however, is generally recognised in Europe, and it was doubtless a knowledge of this fact that induced Great Britain to make such unusual exertions to ally itself with the United States."

Here, again, is another journalistic straw floating on the stream:

" Referring to the fact that English and American officers had fallen side by side in Samoa while promoting commercial interests, Lord [Charles] Beresford expressed the hope that the two nations would ' always be found working and fighting in unison.' This might keep us pretty busy, your lordship."

In a rather low-class farce which I saw in a Chicago theatre, two men wandered through the action, with the charming irrelevance characteristic of American popular drama, attired, one as John Bull, the other as Brother Jonathan. There came a point in the action where some one had to be kicked out of the house. " You do it, Jonathan," said John Bull; whereupon Jonathan retorted: " I know your game; you want me to do your fighting for you, but I *don't do it!* See?" These are ridiculous trifles, no doubt, but they might be indefinitely multiplied; and they show the set of a certain current in American feeling. Let us beware of lending added strength to this current by any appearance of self-interested eagerness in our advances towards America.

One thing we cannot too clearly realise, and that is that the true American clings above everything to his Americanism. The status of an American citizen is to him the proudest on earth, and that [1 although he may clearly enough recognise the abuses of American political life, and the dangers which the Republic has to encounter. The feeling (which is not to be confounded with an ignorant chauvinism, though in some cases it may take that form) is the fundamental feeling of the whole nation; and no emotion which threatened to encroach upon it, or compete with it in any way, would have the least chance of taking a permanent place in the American mind. The feeling which, as one may reasonably hope, is now growing up between the two nations must be based on the mutual admission of absolute independence and equality. The relation is new to history, and must beget a new emotion. Strong as is the bond of mutual interest, it must have a large idealism to reinforce it—a sentiment (shall we say ?) of mutual admiration—if the English-speaking peoples are to play the great part in the drama of the future which Destiny seems to be urging upon them. In order to stand together in perfect freedom and dignity, it is essential that each of the brother-nations should be incontestably able to stand alone. If we want to cement the Anglo-American understanding, the first thing we have to do is to cement the British Empire.

There is no more typical and probably no more widely respected American at the present moment than Governor Roosevelt, of New York. Even those who dissent from his " strenuous " ideal and his expansionist opinions, admit him to be a model of political integrity and public spirit. In an article on "The Monroe Doctrine," published in 1896, Mr. Roosevelt wrote as follows:

"No English colony now stands on a footing of genuine equality with the parent State. As long as the Canadian remains a colonist, he remains in a position which is distinctly inferior to that of his cousins, both in England and in the United States. The Englishman at bottom looks down on the Canadian, as he does on any one who admits his inferiority, and quite properly too. The American, on the other hand, with equal propriety, regards the Canadian with the good-natured condescension always felt by the freeman for the man who is not free. A funny instance of the English attitude towards Canada was shown after Lord Dunraven's inglorious fiasco last September, when the Canadian yachtsman Rose challenged for the America Cup. The English journals repudiated him on the express ground that a Canadian was not an Englishman, and not entitled to the privileges of an Englishman. In their comments, many of them showed a dislike for Americans which almost rose to hatred. The feeling they displayed for Canadians was not one of dislike. It was one of contempt."

There are several contestable points in this statement, and I quote it, though it is but three years old, as a historical rather than a contemporary utterance. At the same time it expresses an almost universal American point of view, and indicates errors to be corrected, dangers to be avoided. It is absurd, of course, that the American should look down upon the Canadian as a " man who is not free "; but every shadow of an excuse for such an attitude ought to be removed, and the citizen of the British Empire ought to have as clearly defined a status as the citizen of the American Republic.

Even if such unpleasant incidents should recur as those to which Mr. Roosevelt alludes, we may trust with tolerable confidence that he would now find no "hatred" for America, or "contempt" for Canada, in the tone of the British Press. The years which have passed since 1896 have not only created a new feeling between England and America, but have drawn the Empire together. In this respect—in every respect—much remains to be done. But at least we can say with assurance that a good beginning has been made towards that consolidation of the English-speaking countries on which the well-being of the world so largely depends.

POSTSCRIPT. — The notion of inevitable hostility between a constitutional Monarchy and a Republic has been fostered by American writers in whom one would have expected greater clearness of perception. We find Lowell, for instance, writing in his well-known essay ***On a Certain Condescension in Foreigners:*** " I never blamed her (England) for not wishing well to democracy—how should she ? " The more obvious question is, How should not one democracy wish another well? There may have been at the time when Lowell wrote, and there may even be to-day, a handful of royalty-worshippers in England who regard a Republic as a vulgar, unpicturesque form of government; but this is not a political opinion, or even preju-dice, but mere stolid snobbery. Whatever were England's misdemeanours towards America at the time of the Civil War, they were not prompted by any hatred of democracy.

I find the same misconception insisted on in a document much later than Low-ell's essay: a leaflet by the Rev. Edward Everett Hale, contributed to a ***Good Citi-zenship Series*** specially designed for the enlightenment of the more ignorant class of American voters. The tract is called ***The Ruhr of America,*** and sets forth that the Ruler of America is " the People with a very large P." Now, according to Dr. Hale, we benighted Europeans are absolutely incapable of grasping this truth. He says : " This is at bottom the trouble with the diplomatists of Europe, with prime ministers, and with leaders of "Er Majesty's Hopposition.'…Even men of intelligence…can make nothing of the central truth of our system…In my house, once, an English gentleman of great intelligence told me that he had visited the White House, and was most glad to pay his respects to 'the Ruler of our Great Nation.' Poor man! he thought he would please me! But he saw his mistake soon enough. I stormed out, 'Ruler of America? Who told you he was the ruler of America ? He never told you so. He is the First Servant of America., And I hope the poor traveller learned his lesson."

It is true that the poor traveller used a pompous and rather absurd expression ; but if he had had his wits about him he might have reminded Dr. Hale that the

President is much more effectively the Ruler of America than the Queen is the Ruler of England. He rules by the direct mandate of the People, but he rules none the less. It would greatly conduce to a just understanding between America and England if the political instructors of the American people would correct instead of confirming the prevalent impression that they have a monopoly of democracy.

GREAT BRITAIN and the United States are sister Commonwealths, enjoying the advantages and exposed to the dangers of sisterhood. The dangers are as real, though we trust not as great, as the advantages. Family quarrels are apt to be the bitterest; a chance word will seem unkind and unbearable from a near kinsman, which, coming from a stranger, would carry no sting at all. As Lowell very truly said, " The common blood, and still more the common language, are fatal instruments of misapprehension." But behind this statement there lies a far deeper though still obvious truth. We misunderstand because we understand; and it would be an extravagance of pessimism to doubt that, in the long run, understanding will carry the day. Light may dazzle here and bewilder there; but, after all, it is light and not darkness. We English and Americans hold a talisman that makes us at home over half, and more than half, the world; and we are not going to rob it of its virtue by renouncing our ties, and wantonly declaring ourselves aliens to each other.

Our unity of speech is such a commonplace that we scarcely notice it. But, rightly regarded, it is a thing to be rejoiced in with a great joy, and not without a certain sense of danger happily escaped. He would have been a bold man who should confidently have prophesied at the Revolution that American and English would remain the same tongue, and that at the end of the nineteenth century there would not be the slightest perceptible cleavage, or threat of ultimate divergence. No doubt there were forces obviously tending to preserve the linguistic unity of the two nations. There was the English Bible for one thing, and there was the whole body of English literature. The Americans, it might have been said, could scarcely be so foolish as deliberately to renounce their spiritual birthright, or let it drift little by little away from them. But, on the other hand, virulent and inveterate political emnity, had it arisen, might quite conceivably have led the Americans to make it a point of honour to differentiate their speech from ours, as many Norwegians are at this moment making it a point of honour to differentiate their language from the Danish, which was until of late years the generally accepted medium of literary expression. In the evolution of their literature, the Americans might purposely have rejected our classical tradition, making their effort rather to depart from than to adhere to it. Again, an observer in 1776 could not have foreseen the practical annihilation, by steam and electricity, of that barrier which then appeared so formidable—the Atlantic Ocean. He might have foreseen the immense influx of men of every race and tongue into the unpeopled West; but he could scarcely have anticipated with confidence the ready absorption of all these alien elements (save one I) into the dominant Anglo-Saxon polity. It was quite on the cards that a new American language might have developed from a fusion of all the diverse tongues of all the scattered races of the earth.

Nothing of the sort, as we know, has happened. The instinct of kinship from the first kept political enmity in check; the Atlantic has been practically wiped out; and English has easily absorbed, in America, all the other idioms which have been brought into contact, rather than competition, with it. The result is that the English language occupies a unique position among the tongues of the earth. It is unique in two dimensions—in altitude and in expanse. It soars to the highest heights of human utterance, and it covers an unequalled area of the earth's surface. Undoubtedly it is the most precious heirloom of our race, and as such we must reverence and guard it. Nor must we islanders talk as though we held it in fee-simple, and allowed our trans-atlantic kinsfolk merely a conditional usufruct of it. Their property in it is as complete and indefeasible as our own; and we should rejoice to accept their aid in the conservation and renovation (equally indispensable processes) of this superb and priceless heritage.

English critics of the beginning of the century so convincingly set forth the reasons why America, absorbed in the conquest of nature and in material progress, could not produce anything great in the way of literature, that their arguments remain embedded in many minds even to this day, when events have conclusively falsified them. It is a commonplace with some people that America has not developed a great *American* literature. If this merely means that, in casting off her allegiance to George III., America did not cast off her allegiance to Chaucer, Shakespeare, Milton, Dryden, Addison, Swift, Pope, the reproach, if it be one, must be accepted. If it be a humiliation to American authors to own the traditions and standards established by these men, and thereby to enrol themselves in their immortal fellowship, why, then it must be owned that they have deliberately incurred that humiliation. One American of vivid originality tried to escape it, and with what result ? Simply that Whitman holds a place of his own, somewhat like that of Blake one might say, in the literature of the English language, and has produced at least as much effect in England as in America. If, on the other hand, it be implied that American literature feebly imitates English literature, and fails to present an original and adequate interpretation of American life, no reproach could well be more flagrantly unjust. It is not only the abstract merit of American literature, though that is very high, but precisely the Americanism of it, that gives it its value in the eyes of all thinking Englishmen. Only one American author of the first rank could possibly, at a superficial glance, appear—not so much English as—European, cosmopolitan. I mean, of course, Edgar Allen Poe, who has left perhaps a deeper impress upon literature outside the English-speaking countries than any other imaginative writer of the century, with the exception of Byron. Poe was, a born idealist, a creature of pure intelligence. Whether in poetry or fiction, he was always solving problems; and it is hard to be distinctively national in an exercise of pure intelligence. We do not look for local colour in, for example, the agreeable essays of Euclid. But Poe's intelligence was, at bottom, of a characteristically American type. He was the Edison of romance.[13] As for the other great writers of America, what can be more patent than their Americanism ? Speaking only, for the present, of those who have joined the majority, I would name two who seem to me to stand with Poe in the very front rank of original genius. They are Emerson, that star like spirit, dwelling in a serener ether than

[13] I went to see Poe's grave in Baltimore, marked by a mean and ugly monument, little more than a mere tombstone. It is surely time that a worthy memorial should be raised, at his burial-place or elsewhere, to this unique genius. England and the English-speaking world would gladly contribute. For a masterly criticism and vindication of Poe, let me refer the reader to

Mr. John M. Robertson's ***New Essays towards a Critical Method.*** London and New York: J. Lane. 1897.

ours, which, though we may never attain, it is yet a refreshment to look up to; and Hawthorne, not perhaps the greatest romancer in the English tongue, but certainly the purest artist in that sphere of fiction. Now, it is a mere truism to say that each of these men was, in his way, a typical product of New England, inconceivable as the offspring of any other soil in the world Emerson, it has been said, not without truth, was the first of the American humourists, carrying into metaphysics that gift of realistic vision and inspired hyperbole which has somehow been grafted upon the Anglo-Saxon character by the conditions of American life. As for Hawthorne, though he has felt and reproduced the physical charm of Rome more subtly than any other artist, his genius drew at once its strength and its delicacy from his Puritan ancestry and environment. To realise how intimately he smacks of the soil, we have but to think of that marvellous scene in ***The Blithe-dale Romance,*** the search for Zenobia's body. From what does it derive its peculiar quality, its haunting savour ? Simply from the presence of Silas Foster, that delightful incarnation of the New England yeoman. " If I thought anything had happened to Zenobia, I should feel kind o' sorrowful," said the grim Silas; and there never was a speech more dramatically true, or, in its context, more bitterly pathetic.

Even while English critics were proving that there could be no such thing as an American literature, Washington Irving and Fenimore Cooper were laying its foundations on a thoroughly American basis. Irving was none the less American for loving the picturesque traditions of his English ancestry; Cooper, a gallant and fertile genius, did his country and our language an inestimable service by adding a whole group of specifically American figures to the deathless aristocracy of the realms of romance. Then, in the generation which has just passed away, we have such men as Thoreau, racy of his native soil; Longfellow, in his day and way the chief interpreter of America to England ; Whittier, so intensely local that, as Professor Matthews puts it, " he wrote for New England rather than for the whole of the United States "; Lowell, courtly, cultured, cosmopolitan, and yet the creator of Hosea Biglow; Holmes, as American in his humour as Lamb was English, who justly ranks with Lamb and Goldsmith among the personally best-beloved writers of the English tongue. Prescott, in the sphere of history, paralleled the achievement of Cooper in fiction, by giving literary form to the romance of the New World; while Motley was inspired (too ardently perhaps) by the spirit of free America in writing the great epic of religious and political freedom in Europe. Finally, it must not be forgotten that in **Uncle Tom's Cabin,** a tragically American production, Mrs. Beecher Stowe added to the literature of the English language the most potent, the most dynamic, pamphlet ever hurled into the arena of national life.

Of all that living Americans are doing for the literature of our common tongue it is as yet impossible to speak adequately. Since 1870 a new spirit of nationalism has entered into American literature, which has not yet been thoroughly studied in America or appreciated in England. So far from having no national literature, America has now, perhaps, the most intimately national body of fiction in the modern world. Before the Civil War there was practically no deliberate and systematic study of local and racial idiosyncrasies. Hosea Biglow was a mask, not a character, and Parson Wilbur was a literary device. Even Hawthorne thought primarily of the element of imagination in his romances—the universal, not the local, element. His leading characters are psychological creations, with nothing specifically American about them; his local colour and local character-study, though admirable, are incidental, or at any rate stand on a secondary plane. In the South there was no literature at all, local or otherwise, with the one startling exception of **Uncle Tom's Cabin.** [14] But since 1870, and mainly, indeed, within the past twenty years, a marvellous change has come over the scene. Not only the national but the local self-consciousness of America has sprung to literary life, until at the present day there is scarcely a corner of the country, scarcely an

[14] For the reasons of this barrenness, see an essay on **Two Studies in the South** in Professor Brander Matthews's **Aspects of Fiction.** New York : Harper. 1896.

aspect of social life, that has not found its special, and, as a rule, very able interpreter through the medium of fiction. Pursuing technical methods partly borrowed from abroad (from France rather than from England), American writers have undertaken what one is tempted to call a sociological ordnance-survey of the Republic from Maine to Arizona, from Florida to Oregon. There is scarcely a human being in the United States, from the Newport society belle to the " greaser " of New Mexico, that has not his or her more or less faithful counterpart in fiction. No European country, so far as I know, has achieved anything like such comprehensive self-realisation. Comprehensive, I say—not necessarily profound. Perhaps France in Balzac, perhaps Russia in Turgueneff and Tolstoi, found more searching interpretation than America has found even in her host of novelists. But never, surely, was there a body of fiction that touched life at so many points, to mirror if not to probe it. And in many cases to probe it as well.

It would take a volume to criticise these writers in any detail. I can attempt no more than a bald and imperfect enumeration. Miss Mary Wilkins's studies of New England life are well known and appreciated in England, but the talent of Miss Sarah Orne Jewitt is not sufficiently recognised. In her *Country of the Pointed Firs,* for example, there are whole chapters that rise to a classical perfection of workmanship. The novelists of the Eastern cities, with Mr. Howells, a master craftsman, at their head, are of course numberless. For studies in the local colour of New York nothing could be better than Mr. Brander Matthews's *Vignettes of Manhattan,* and other stories. Mr. Paul Leicester Ford's *Honorable Peter Stirling,* though antiquated in style, gives a remarkable picture of political life in New York. The Bowery Boy is cleverly represented, so far as dialect at any rate is concerned, by Mr. E. W. Towns-end in his *Chimmie Fadden.* Even the Jewish and the Italian quarters of New York have their portraitists in fiction. Life in Washington has been frequently and ably depicted; for instance, in Mrs. Burnett's *Through one Administration.* Of the many interpreters of the South I need mention only three: Mr. Cable, Mr. Thomas Nelson Page, and Mr. Chandler Harris. Miss Murfree (" Charles Egbert Craddock") has made the Mountains of Tennessee her special province. Chicago has several novelists of her own: for example, Mr. Henry Fuller, author of *The Cliff Dwellers,* Mr. Will Payne, and that close student of Chicago slang, Mr. George Ade, the author of Artie. The Middle West counts such novelists as Miss " Octave

Thanet" and Mr. Hamlin Garland, whose **Main Travelled Roads** contains some very remarkable work. The Far West is best represented, perhaps, in the lively and graphic sketches of Mr. Owen Wister; while California has novelists of talent in Miss Gertrude Atherton and Mr. Frank Norris. At least two Americans living abroad have made noteworthy contributions to this sociological survey of their native land: the late Mr. Harold Frederic, who has dealt mainly with country life in New York State, and Miss Elizabeth Robins, whose picture, in **The Open Question,** of a Southern family impoverished by the war, is exceedingly vivid and bears all the marks of the utmost fidelity. Nor must I omit to mention that the stage has borne a modest but not insignificant part in this movement of national self-portraiture. Mr. Augustus Thomas's **Alabama** is a delightful picture of Southern life, while Mr. James A. Heme's **Shore** Acres takes a distinct place in the literature of New England, his **Griffith Davenport** [15] in the literature of Virginia.

There must, of course, be many gaps in this summary enumeration. It is very probable that many novelists of distinction have altogether escaped my notice; and I have made no attempt to include in my list the writers of short magazine stories, many of them artists of high accomplishment. One omission, however, I must at once repair. " Mark Twain's " contributions to the work of self-realisation have been in the main retrospective, but nevertheless of the first importance. He is the " sacred poet" of the Mississippi. If any work of incontestable genius, and plainly predestined to immortality, has been issued in the English language during the past quarter of a century, it is that

[15] Founded on a novel by Miss Helen H. Gardener.

brilliant romance of the Great Rivers, **The Adventures of Huckleberry Finn.**

Intensely American though he be, " Mark Twain" is one of the greatest living masters of the English language. To some Englishmen this may seem a paradox; but it is high time we should disabuse ourselves of the prejudice that residence on the European side of the Atlantic confers upon us an exclusive right to determine what is good English, and to write it correctly and vigorously. We are apt in England to class as an " Americanism " every unfamiliar, or too familiar, locution which we do not happen to like. As a matter of fact, there is a pretty lively interchange between the two countries of slipshod and vulgar "journalese"; and as the picturesque reporter is a greater power in America than he is with us, we perhaps import more than we export of this particular commodity. But there can be no rational doubt, I think, that the English language has gained, and is gaining, enormously by its expansion over the American continent. The prime function of a language, after all, is to interpret the " form and pressure " of life—the experience, knowledge, thought, emotion, and aspiration of the race which employs it. This being so, the more taproots a language sends down into the soil of life, and the more varied the strata of human experience from which it draws its nourishment, whether of vocabulary or idiom, the more perfect will be its potentialities as a medium of expression. We must be careful, it is true, to keep the organism healthy, to guard against disintegration of tissue ; but to that duty American writers are quite as keenly alive as we. It is not a source of weakness but of power and vitality to the English language that it should embrace a greater variety of dialects than any other civilised tongue. A new language, says the proverb, is a new sense; but a multiplicity of dialects means, for the possessors of the main language, an enlargement of the pleasures of the linguistic sense without the fatigue of learning a totally new grammar and vocabulary. So long as there is a potent literary tradition keeping the core of the language one and indivisible, vernacular variations can only tend, in virtue of the survival of the fittest, to promote the abundance, suppleness, and nicety of adaptation of the language as a literary instrument. The English language is no mere historic monument, like Wesf-minster Abby, to be religiously preserved as a relic of the past, and reverenced as the burial-place of a bygone breed of giants. It is a living organism, ceaselessly busied, like any other organism, in the processes of assimilation and excretion. It has before it, we may fairly hope, a future still greater than its glorious past. And the greatness of that future will largely depend on the harmonious interplay of spiritual forces throughout the American Republic and the British Empire.

THE AMERICAN LANGUAGE

NOTHING short of an imperative sense of duty could tempt me to set forth on that most perilous emprise, a discussion of the American language. The path is beset with man-traps and spring-guns. Not all the serious causes of dissension between England and America have begotten half the bad blood that has been engendered by trumpery questions of vocabulary, grammar, and pronunciation. I cannot hope to escape giving offence, probably on both sides; but if I can induce one or two people on either side to think twice before they scoff once, I shall not have written in vain.

In the way of scoffing, we English have doubtless (and inevitably) been the worst offenders. We have habitually used " Americanism " as a term of reproach, implying, if not saying in so many words, that America was the great source of pollution, and of nothing but pollution, to the otherwise limpid current of our speech. Dean Alford wrote offensively to this effect; Archbishop Trench, on the other hand, discussed the relations between the English of America and the English of England with courtesy and good sense. (See ***English Past and Present,*** ninth edition, pp. 63, 215.) He protested against certain transatlantic neologisms, including in his list that excellent old word " to berate," and a word so useful and so eminently consonant with the spirit of the language as " to belittle"; but, whether wise or unwise, his protest was at least civil. Other writers, both in books and periodicals, have been apt to take their tone from the Dean rather than from the Archbishop. It may even be said that the instinct of the majority of Englishmen, which finds heedless expression in the newspapers and common talk, is to regard Americanisms as necessarily vulgar, and (conversely) vulgarisms as probably American. If challenged and brought to book, they can generally realise the narrowness and injustice of this way of thinking; yet they relapse into it next moment. It is time we should be on our guard against so insidious a .habit. Its reduction to absurdity may be found (alackaday!) in ***Fors Clavigera*** for June I, 1874. With shame and sorrow I transcribe the passage, for the time has not yet come for it to be forgotten. If it were merely the aberration of an individual, however distinguished, it were better kept out of sight, out of mind; but it is, I repeat, the reckless exaggeration of a not altogether uncommon habit of thought:

" England taught the Americans all they have of speech or thought, hitherto. What thoughts they have not learned from England are foolish thoughts; what words they have not learned from England, unseemly words; the vile among them not being able even to be humorous parrots, but only obscene mocking-birds."

Can we wonder that Americans have retorted with some asperity upon criticisms in which any approach to such insolent insularism is even remotely or inadvertently implied ?

The American retort, however, has not always been judicious or dignified. It has too often consisted in the mere pitting of one linguistic prejudice against another. It is very easy to prove that there are bad speakers and bad writers in both countries, and the attempt to determine which country has the more numerous and the greater sinners is exceedingly unprofitable. The " You're another " style of argument has been far too prevalent. Here we have Mr. Gilbert M. Tucker, for instance, in a book entitled ***Our Common Speech*** (1895) implying, if he does not absolutely assert (p. 173), that a "boldness of innovation " in matters linguistic, amounting to "absolute licentiousness," is more characteristic of England than of America. The suggestion leaves my British withers entirely unwrung, for I approve of bold innovation in language, trusting to the impermanence of the unfit to counteract the effects of licentiousness. If I could believe that we British were the bolder innovators, I should admit it without blenching; but observation and probability seem to me to point with one accord in the opposite direction. New words are begotten by new conditions of life; and as American life is far more fertile of new conditions than ours, the tendency towards neologism cannot but be stronger in America than in England. America has enormously enriched the language, not only with new words, but (since the American mind is, on the whole, quicker and wittier than the English) with apt and luminous colloquial metaphors; and I know not why Mr. Tucker should disclaim the credit. He next sets forth to show how recent English writers are corrupting the language; and, in doing so, he falls into some curious errors. Dickens was boldly innovating when he made Silas Wegg say, "Mr. Boffin, I never bargain"—"haggle," it would seem, is the proper word. But if Mr. Tucker will look into the matter, he will find it extremely probable that this was the original sense of the word " bargain," and quite certain that it was a very early sense; for instance—

> So worthless peasants bargain for their wives,
> As market-men for oxen, sheep, or horse.
> I HENRY VI., V. v. 53.

And, in any case, is it possible to set up such a distinction between " bargaining" and "haggling" as to be worth an international wrangle ? " Starved" for frozen is to Mr. Tucker an innovation; it was used both by Shakespeare and Milton. " Assist" in the sense of to " be present at" is an " absurd " innovation; it was used by Gibbon and by Prescott, a " tolerably good authority," says Mr. Tucker himself, " in the use of English." Miss Yonge is taken to task for saying, " Theodora *flung* away and was rushing off"; but Milton says, "And crop-full out of doors he flings." Charles Reade " is guilty of such phrases as 'Wardlaw whipped before him,' 'Ransome whipped before it'"; but the Princess in ***Love's Labour's Lost*** is guilty of saying, " Whip to our tents, as roes run o'er the land," and the word occurs in the same sense in Ben Jonson and Steele, to search no further. The simple fact is that Mr. Tucker has not happened to note the intransitive sense of " to fling" and "to whip," which has been current in the best authors for centuries. He is very severe on the English habit of " inserting utterly superfluous words," instancing from Lord Beacons- field, " He was ***by way of*** intimating that he was engaged on a great work," and, from a magazine, "She was ***by way of*** painting the shrimp girl." Now, this is not an elegant expression, and for my part I should be at some pains to avoid it; but it has a perfectly distinct meaning, and is not a mere redundancy. If Mr. Tucker supposes that " She was by way of painting the shrimp girl" means exactly the same as "She was painting the shrimp girl," he misses one of the fine shades of the English language. Similarly, his remark on the " peculiar misuse of the affix ***ever***, as in saying ' Whatever are you doing ?'" stands in need of reconsideration. It is wrong, certainly, to treat ***ever*** as an affix, and to mistake the first two words of ' What ever are you doing ?'" for the one word " whatever "; but to suppose the "ever" meaningless and inert is to overlook a clearly marked and very useful gradation of emphasis. "What are you doing ? " expresses simple curiosity; " What ever are you doing ? " expresses surprise; "What the devil are you doing?" expresses anger —we need not run farther up the scale. Nor is this use of " ever " an innovation, licentious or otherwise. "Ever" has for centuries been employed as an intensive particle after the interrogative pronouns and adverbs how, who, what, where, why. For instance, in *The World of Wonders* (I607), "I shall desire him to consider how ever it was possible to get an answer from these priests."

One of the most remarkable paragraphs in Mr. Tucker's book is that in which he proves "the greater permanence and steadiness of our American speech as compared with that of the mother country " by going through Halliwell's *Dictionary of Archaisms and Provincialisms* and picking out 76 words which Halliwell regards as obsolete, but which in America are all alive and kicking. (The vulgarism is mine, not Mr. Tucker's.) Now as a matter of fact not one of these words is really obsolete in England, and most of them are in everyday use; for instance, adze, affectation, agape, to age, air (appearance), appellant, applepie order, baker's dozen, bamboozle, bay window, between whiles, bicker, blanch, to brain, burly, catcall, clodhopper, clutch, coddle, copious, cosy, counterfeit money, crazy (dilapidated), crone, crook, croon, cross-grained, cross-patch, cross purposes, cuddle, to cuff, cleft, din, earnest money, egg on, greenhorn, jack-of-all-trades, loophole, settled, ornate, to quail, ragamuffin, riff-raff, rigmarole, scant, seedy, out of sorts, stale, tardy, trash. How Halliwell ever came to class these words as archaic I cannot imagine; but I submit that any one who sets forth to write about the English of England ought to have sufficient acquaintance with the language to check and reject Halliwell's amazing classification. Does Mr. Tucker so despise British English as never to read an English book ? How else is one to account for his imagining for a moment that clodhopper, clutch, copious, cosy, cross-grained, greenhorn, and rigmarole are obsolete in England ?

Far be it from me to assert that Mr. Tucker makes no good points in his catalogue of English solecisms. I merely hint that this game of pot and kettle is neither dignified nor profitable; that purism is almost always over-hasty, and apt to ignore both the history and the psychology of language; and, finally, that nothing is gained by introducing acerbity (though I have admitted the frequent provocation) into a discussion which a little exercise of temper should render no less agreeable than instructive to both parties. "The speech of the lower orders of our people," says Mr. Tucker, "... differs from what all admit to be standard correctness in a much smaller degree[16] than we have every reason to believe to be the case in England, *our enemies themselves being judges.*" Now I protest I am not Mr. Tucker's enemy, and I know of no reason why he should be mine. I cannot share the withering contempt with which he regards the extension of the term " traffic " from barter to movement to and fro, as in a street or on a railway; but if he prefers another word (he does not suggest one, by the way) for the traffic on Broadway or on the New York Central, I shall not esteem him one whit the less. Even when he tells me that "bumper" is the English term for the American " buffer " (on a railway carriage) I do not feel my blood boil. A very slight elevation of the eyebrows expresses all the emotion of which I am conscious. So long as he does not insist on my saying a " bumper state" when I mean a " buffer state," I see no reason whatever for any rupture of that sympathy which ought to subsist between two

[16] " What great city of this country," Mr. Tucker inquires, " has developed, or is likely to develop, any peculiar class of errors at all comparable in importance to those of the Cockney speech of London ? " The answer is pat: New York and Chicago —unless Mr. Townsend's ***Chimmie Fadden*** and Mr. Ade's ***Artie*** are sheer linguistic libels.

It must be very painful to Mr. Tucker to find Shakespeare talking of the " two hours' traffic of our stage." He was a hardened offender, was Shakespeare, against Mr. Tucker's ideal of one single, inelastic, cast-iron signification for every word in the language.

men who take a common interest and pride in the subject of his treatise— ***Our Common Speech.***

II

It is not to be expected that an extremely English intonation should ever be agreeable to Americans, or an extremely American intonation to Englishmen. We ourselves laugh at a " haw-haw " intonation in English; why, then, should we forbid Americans to do so ? If " an accent like a banjo " is recognised as undesirable in America (and assuredly it is), there is no reason why we in England should pretend to admire it. But a vulgar or affected intonation is clearly distinguishable, and ought to be clearly distinguished, from a national habit in the pronunciation of a given letter, or accentuation of a particular word, or class of words. For instance, take the pronounciation of the indefinite article. The American habitually says "a man " (*a* as in "game") ; the Englishman, unless he wants to be emphatic, says, "a man."[17] Neither is right, neither wrong; it is purely a matter of habit; and to consider either habit

> [17] " Surely, on Mr. Archer's own showing" writes Mr. A. B. Walkley, " the Englishman has the advantage here, for ' when he wants to be emphatic' he can be, whereas the American cannot." This is a misapprehension on Mr. Walkley's part. The American ft can be spoken with or without emphasis, just as the speaker pleases. It is because we are accustomed always to associate this particular sonority with emphasis that even when it is spoken without emphasis, we imagine it to be emphatic.

ridiculous is merely to exhibit that childishness or provincialism of mind which is moved to laughter by whatever is unfamiliar. Again, when I first read the works of the sagacious Mr. Dooley, I thought it a curiously far-fetched idea on the part of that philosopher to talk of Admiral Dewey as his " Cousin George," and assert that " Dewey " and " Dooley " were practically the same name. I had not then noticed that the American pronunciation of "Dewey" is "Dooey," and that the liquid "yoo" is very seldom heard in America. In the course of the five minutes I spent in the Supreme Court at Washington, I heard the Chief Justice of the United States make this one remark : " That, sir, is not ***constitootional*** " To our ears this "oo" has an old-fashioned ring, like that of the "ee" in "obleeged "; but to call it wrong is absurd, and to find it ridiculous is provincial. Very possibly it can be proved that had Shakespeare used the word at all, he would have said " constitootional" ; but that would make the " oo" neither better nor worse in my eyes. There always have been, and always will be, changing fashions in pronunciation; and the Americans have as good a right to their fashion as we to ours. Fifty years hence, perhaps, our grandsons will be saying " constitootional, " and theirs " constityootional." I confess that, in point of abstract sonority, I prefer the " yoo " to the dry " oo "; but that, again, is a pure matter of taste. If Americans choose to say,

"From morn To noon he fell, from noon to dooey eve, A summer's day,"

I am perfectly willing that they should do so, reserving always my own right to say "dyooey." It would not at all surprise me to learn that Milton said " dooey " ; but neither would it lead me to altef the pronunciation which, as one of the present generation of Englishmen, I have learnt to prefer.

It is said that when Mr. Daly's company returned to New York, after a long visit to England, they pronounced " lieutenant" according to the English fashion, " leftenant," but were called to order by an outburst of protest. Though, for my own part, I say " leftenant," I heartily sympathise with the protesters. " Leftenant," though a corruption of respectable antiquity, is a corruption none the less, and since it has died out in America, it would be mere snobbery to reintroduce it.

So, too, with questions of accentuation. We say " primarily " and " temporarily "; most (or at any rate many) Americans say " primarily" and " temporarily." Here there is no question of right or wrong, refinement or vulgarity. The one accentuation is as good as the other. It may be argued, indeed, that our accentuation throws into relief the root, the idea, the soul of the word, not the mere grammatical suffix, the "limbs and outward flourishes " ; but on the other hand, it may be contended with equal truth that the American accentuation has the Latin precedent in its favour. Neither advantage is conclusive; neither, indeed, is, strictly speaking, relevant; for Englishmen do not make a principle of accentuating the root rather than the prefix or suffix, else we should say " inundation," " resonant," " admirable "; and the Americans do not make a principle of following the Latin emphasis, else they would say " orator" and " gratuitous," and the recognised pronunciation of " theatre " would be " theayter." It is argued that there is a general tendency among educated Englishmen to throw the accent as far back as possible; that, for instance, the educated speaker says " interesting," the uneducated, "interesting." True ; but until this tendency can be proved to possess some inherent advantage, there is not a shadow of reason why Americans should be reproached or ridiculed for obeying their own tendency rather than ours. The English tendency is a matter of comparatively recent fashion. " Con'template," said Samuel Rogers, " is bad enough, but balcony makes me sick." Both forms have maintained themselves up to the present; but will they for long ? I think one may already trace a reaction against the universal throwing backward of the accent. I myself say " peremptory " and " exemplary "; but it would take very little encouragement to make me say " peremptory " and " exemplary," which seem to me much more expressive words. There is surely no doubt that, in accenting a prefix rather than the root of the word, we lose a certain amount of force. " Contemplate," for instance, is not nearly so strong a word as "contemplate." We says an " illustrated" book or the " *Illustrated London News* ," because we do not require any particular force in the epithet; but when the sense demands a word with colour and emotion in it, we say the " illustrious " statesman, the " illustrious " poet, throwing into relief the essential element in the word, the " lustre." What a paltry word would "triumphant" be in comparison with "triumphant"! But the larger our list of examples, the more capricious does our accentuation seem, the more evidently subject to mere accidents of fashion. There is scarcely a trace of consistent or rational principle in the matter. To make a merit of one practice, and find in the other a subject for contemptuous criticism, is simply childish.

Mere slovenliness of pronunciation is a totally different matter. For instance, the use of " most " for "almost" is distinctly, if not a vulgarism, at least a colloquialism. It may be of ancient origin; it may have crossed in the *Mayflower* for aught I know; but the overwhelming preponderance of ancient and modern usage is certainly in favour of prefixing the " al," and there is a clear advantage in having a special word for this special idea. If American writers tried to make " most " supplant "almost" in the literary language, we should have a right to remonstrate; the two forms would fight it out, and the fittest would survive. But as a matter of fact I am not aware that any one has attempted to introduce "most," in this sense, into literature. It is perfectly recognised as a colloquialism, and as such it keeps its place. Again, such pronunciations as "mebbe" for "maybe "and "I'd ruther" or" I druther" for "I'd rather" are obvious slovenlinesses. No American would defend them as being correct, any more than an Englishman would defend " I dunno " for " I don't know " or " atome " for " at home." If an actor, for instance, were to say,

" I druther be a dog and bay the moon
Than such a Roman,"

American and English critics alike could not but protest against the solecism; for in poetry absolute precision of utterance is clearly indispensable. But in everyday speech a certain amount of colloquialism is inevitable. Let him whose own enunciation is chemically free from localism or slovenliness cast the first stone even at " mebbe " and " ruther."

A curious American colloquialism, of which I certainly cannot see the advantage, is the substitution of " yep " or " yup " for " yes," and of " nope " for " no." No doubt we have in England the costers " yuss "; but one hears even educated Americans now and then using " yep," or some other corruption of "yes," scarcely to be indicated by the ordinary alphabetical symbols. It seems to me a pity.

Much more respectable in point of antiquity is the habit which obtains to some extent, even among educated Americans, of saying " somewheres " and "a long ways." Here the "s" is an old caseending, an adverbial genitive. " He goes out nights," too, on which Mr. Andrew Lang is so severe, is a form as old as the language and older. I turn to Dr. Leon Kellner's *Historical English Syntax* (p. II9) and find that the Gothic for "at night" was " nahts," and that the form (with its correlative "days") runs through old Norse, old Saxon, old English, and middle English: for instance, " dages endi nahtes " (Hêliand), " daeges and nihtes (Beówulf) , "daeies and nihtes" (Layamon), all meaning "by day and by night." In all, or almost all, words ending in " ward," the genitive inflexion, according to modern English practice, can either be retained or dropped at will. It is a mere pedantry to declare " toward " better English than " towards," "upward" than "upwards." Thus we see that here again there is neither logical principle nor consistent practice to be invoked. At the same time, as " somewheres " has become irremediably a vulgarism in England, it would, I think, be a graceful concession on the part of educated Americans to drop the " s." After all, " somewhere " does not jar in America, and " somewheres " very distinctly jars in England.

An insidious laxity of pronunciation (rather than of grammar), which is taking great hold in America, is the total omission of the "had" or "have "in such phrases as "you'd better," "we've got to." Mr. Howells's Willis Campbell, a witty and cultivated Bostonian, says, in **The Albany Depot**, " I guess we better get out of here " ; Mr. Ade's Artie, a Chicago clerk, says, " I got a boost in my pay," meaning " I have got " : the locution is very common indeed. It is no more defensible than " s help me " for " so help me." It arises from sheer laziness, unwillingness to face the infinitesimal difficulty of pronouncing "d" and "b" together. As a colloquialism it is all very well; but I regard it with a certain alarm, for where all trace of a word disappears, people are apt to forget the logical and grammatical necessity for it. Though contracted to its last letter, a word still asserts its existence; but when even the last letter has vanished its state is parlous indeed.

An Anglicism much ridiculed in America is " different to." As a Scotchman I dislike it, and would neither use nor defend it. At the same time I cannot but hint to American critics that the use of a particular preposition in a particular context is largely a matter of convention; that when we learn a new language we have simply to get up by rote the conventions that obtain in this regard, reason being little or no guide to us; and that within the same language the conventions are always changing. You may easily nonplus even a good grammarian by asking him suddenly, " What preposition should you use in such and-such a context ? " just as you may puzzle a man by asking him to spell a word which, if he wrote it without thinking about it, would present no difficulty to him. Some very good American writers always say, " at the North " and " at the South," where an Englishman would certainly say " in." " At," to my mind, suggests a very narrow point of space. I should say " at" a village, but " in " a city—" at Concord," but " in Boston." I recognise, however, that this is a mere matter of convention, and do not dream of condemning " at the North " as an error. In the same way I would claim tolerance, though certainly not approval, for " different to."

As a general rule, I think, educated Americans are more apt to err on the side of purism than of laxity. I have before me, for example, a long list of rules and warnings for American writers, issued by the **New York Press,** many of which are very much to the point, while others seem to me captious and pedantic. For instance, a woman is not to " marry " a man; she is "married to" him; "the clergyman or magistrate marries both." The grammatical suitor, then, when the awful moment arrives, must not say to the blushing fair, " Will you marry me ? " but "Will you be married to me?" Again, you not only must not split infinitives, but you must not separate an auxiliary from its verb ; you must say " probably will be," not " will probably be." This is English by the card indeed.

I will not waste space upon discussing the different fashions of spelling in England and America. The rage excited in otherwise rational human beings by the dropping of the " u" in " favor/' or the final " me" in " program," is one of the strangest of psychological phenomena. The baselessness of the reasonings used to bolster up the British clinging to superfluous letters is very ably shown in Professor Matthews's **Americanisms and Briticisms.** Let me only put in a plea for the retention of such ab-normal spellings as serve to distinguish two words of the same sound. For instance, it seems to me useful that we should write " story " for a tale and " storey " for a floor, and in the plural " stories" and " storeys."

III

Passing now from questions of pronunciation and grammar to questions of vocabulary, I can only express my sense of the deep indebtedness of the English language, both literary and colloquial, to America for the old words she has kept alive and the new words and phrases she has invented. It is a sheer pedantry—nay, a misconception of the laws which govern language as a living organism—to despise pithy and apt colloquialisms, and even slang. In order to remain healthy and vigorous, a literary language must be rooted in the soil of a copious vernacular, from which it can extract and assimilate, by a chemistry peculiar to itself, whatever nourishment it requires. It must keep in touch with life in the broadest acceptation of the word; and life at certain levels, obeying a psychological law which must simply be accepted as one of the conditions of the problem, will always express itself in dialect, provincialism, slang.

America doubles and trebles the number of points at which the English language comes in touch with nature and life, and is therefore a great source of strength and vitality. The literary language, to be sure, rejects a great deal more than it absorbs; and even in the vernacular, words and expressions are always dying out and being replaced by others which are somehow better adapted to the changing conditions. But though an expression has not, in the long run, proved itself fitted to survive, it does not follow that it has not done good service in its time. Certain it is that the common speech of the Anglo-Saxon race throughout the world is exceedingly supple, well nourished, and rich in forcible and graphic idioms; and a great part of this wealth it owes to America. Let the purists who sneer at " Americanisms " think for one moment how much poorer the English language would be to-day if North America had become a French or Spanish instead of an English continent.

I am far from advocating a breaking down of the barrier between literary and vernacular speech. It should be a porous, a permeable bulwark, allowing of free filtration; but it should be none the less distinct and clearly recognised. Nor do I recommend an indiscriminate hospitality to all the linguistic inspirations of the American fancy. All I say is that neologisms should be judged on their merits, and not rejected with contumely for no better reason than that they are new and (presumably) American. Take, for instance, the word "scientist." It was originally suggested by Whewell in I840; but it first came into common use in America, and was received in England at the point of the bayonet. Huxley and other " scientists " disowned it, and only a few years ago the ***Daily News*** denounced it as " an ignoble

Americanism," a " cheap and vulgar product of transatlantic slang." But " scientist" is undoubtedly holding its own, and will soon be as generally accepted as "retrograde," "reciprocal," "spurious," and "strenuous," against which Ben Jonson, in his day, so—strenuously protested. It holds its own because it is felt to be a necessity. No one who is in the habit of writing will pretend that it is always possible to fall back upon the cumbrous phrase " man of science."[18] On the other hand, the purist objection to " scientist "—

[18] Mr. Andrew Lang says : "Plenty of other words are formed on the same analogy: the Greeks, in the verb ' to Medize,' set the example. But we happen to have no use for • scientist.' " It is not quite clear whether Mr. Lang employs " have no use " in the American sense, expressing sheer dislike, or in the literal and English sense. In the latter case I can only say that he has been fortunate in never coming across conjunctures in which " man of science" came in awkwardly and inelegantly.

that it is a Latin word with a Greek termination, and that it implies the existence of a non-existent verb—may be urged with equal force against such harmless necessary words as deist, aurist, dentist, florist, jurist, oculist, somnambulist, ventriloquist, and—purist. Much more valid objection might be made to the word " scientific," which is not hybrid indeed, but is, if strictly examined, illogical and even nonsensical. The fact is that three-fourths of the English language would crumble away before a purist analysis, and we should be left without words to express the commonest and most necessary ideas.

Contrast with the case of " scientist" a vulgarism such as the use of " transpire" in the sense of " happen." I do not quote it as an Americanism ; it is probably of English origin; it occurs, I regret to note, in Dickens. I select it merely as an example of a demonstrably vicious locution which ought indubitably to be banished from the language. It has its origin in sheer blundering. Some one, at some time, has come upon the phrase " such-and-such a thing has transpired"—that is, leaked out, become known—and, ignorantly mistaking its meaning, has noted and employed the word as a finer-sounding synonym for " occurred " or " happened." The blunder has been passed on from one penny-a-liner to another, until at last it has crept into the pages of writers, on both sides of the Atlantic, who ought to know better. If it served any purpose, expressed any shade of meaning, it might be tolerated; but being at once a useless pedantry and an obvious blunder, it deserves no quarter.

My point, then, is that " scientist" ought to live on its merits, " transpire " to die on its demerits. With regard to every neologism we ought first to inquire, " Does it fill a gap ? Does it serve a purpose ? " And if that question be answered in the affirmative, we may next consider whether it is formed on a reasonably good analogy and in consonance with the general spirit of the language. " Truthful," for example, is said to be an Americanism, and at one time gave offence on that account. It is not only a vast improvement on the stilted " veracious," but one of the prettiest and most thoroughly English words in the dictionary.

The above-quoted writer in the **New York Press** is a purist in vocabulary, no less than in grammar. He will not allow us to be " unwell," we must always be " ill"; an inhuman imperative. Why should we sacrifice this clear and useful gradation : unwell, very unwell, ill, very ill ? On " sick " he does not deliver judgment. The American use of the word is ancient and respectable, but the English limitation of its meaning seems to me convenient, seeing we have the general terms " unwell" and " ill" ready to hand.. Again, the **New York Press** authority follows Freeman in wishing to eject the word " ovation " from the language; surely a ridiculous literalism. It is true we do not sacrifice a sheep at a modern " ovation," but neither (for example) do we judge by the flight of birds when we declare the circumstances to be "auspicious" for such and such an undertaking. Again, we are never to "retire" for the night, but always to " go to bed." If, as is commonly alleged, Americans say " retire " because they consider it indelicate to go to bed, the feeling and the expression are alike foolish. But I do not believe that either is at all common in America. On the other hand, one may retire for the night without going to bed. In the case of ladies especially, the interval between retiring and going to bed is reputed to be far from inconsiderable. If, then, one really means " retired for the night" and does not definitely mean " went to bed," I see no crime in employing the expression that conveys one's exact meaning. Finally the -New York Press will not let us use the word " commence " ; we must always " begin." This is an excellent example of unreflecting or half-reflecting purism. " Commence " is a very old word; it is used by the best writers; it is easily pronounceable and not in the least grandiloquent; indeed it has precisely the length and cadence of its competitor. But somebody or other one day observed that it was Latin, whereas " begin " was Saxon; and since then there has been a systematic attempt, in several quarters, to hound the innocent and useful synonym out of the language. Whence comes this rage for impoverishing our tongue! The more synonyms we possess the better. Wherefore (by the way) I for my part should not be too rigorous in excluding a forcible Americanism merely because it happens to duplicate some word or expression already current in England. The rich language is that which possesses not only the necessaries of life but also an abundance of superfluities.

IV

Let me note a few of the Americanisms, good, bad, and indifferent, which specially struck me, whether in talk or in books, during my recent visit to the United States. I call them Americanisms without inquiring into their history. Some of them may be of English origin; but for practical purposes an Americanism may be taken to mean an expression commonly used in America and not commonly used in England.

I had not been three hours on American soil before I heard a charming young lady remark, " Oh, it was bully " I gathered that this expression is considered admissible, in the conversation of grown-up people, only in and about New York. I often heard it there, and never anywhere else. A very distinguished officer, who served as a volunteer in Cuba, was asked to state his impressions of war. "War," he said, "is a terrible thing. You can't exaggerate its horrors. When you sit in your tent the night before the battle, and think of home and your wife and children, you feel pretty sick and downhearted. But," he added, "next day, when you're in it, oh, it is bully!"

The general use of picturesque metaphor is of course a striking feature in American conversation. Many of these expressions have taken firm root in England, such as " to have no use for" a man, or " to take no stock in " a theory. But fresh inventions crop up on every hand in America. For instance, where an English theatrical manager would say, " We must get this play well talked about and paragraphed in advance," an American manager puts the whole thing much more briefly and forcibly in the phrase, " We don't want this piece to come in on · rubbers." Metaphor apart, many Americans have a gift of fantastic extravagance of phrase which often produces an irresistible effect. A gentleman in high political office had one day to receive a deputation with whose objects he had no sympathy. He listened for some time to the spokesman of the party, and then, at a pause, broke in with the remark : "Gentlemen, you need proceed no further. I am not an entirely dishevelled jackass ! " One would give something for a snapshot photograph of the faces of that deputation.

Small differences of expression (other than those with which every one is familiar—such as " elevator," "baggage," "depot," —strike one in daily life. The American for " To let" is " For rent" ; a " thing one would wish to have expressed otherwise " is, more briefly, " a bad break"; instead of "He married money" an American will say "He married rich "; but this, I take it, is a vulgarism— as, indeed, is the English expression. I find that in the modern American novel, setting forth the sayings and doings of more or less educated people, there are apt to be, on an average, about half a dozen words and phrases at which the English reader stumbles for a moment. Mr. Howells, a master of English, may be taken as a faithful reporter of the colloquial speech of Boston and New York. In one of his comediettas, he makes Willis Campbell say, " Let me turn out my sister's cup " (pour her a cup of tea). Mrs. Roberts, in another of these delightful little pieces, says, " I'll smash off a note," where an English Mrs. Roberts would say "dash off"; and where an English Mrs. Roberts would ring the bell, her American namesake " touches the annunciator." It is commonly believed in England that there is no such thing as a " servant" in America, i but only " hired girls" and " helps." This is certainly not so in New York. I once "rang up" a friend's house by telephone, and, on asking 5 who was speaking to me, received the answer in a feminine voice, " I'm one of Mr. So-and-so's servants."

The heroine of ***The Story of a Play*** says to her husband, " Are you still thinking of our scrap of this morning? " " Scrap," in the sense of " quarrel," is one of the few exceedingly common American expressions which have as yet taken little hold in England.[19] Admiral Dewey, for instance, is admired as a " scrapper," or, as we should phrase it, a fighting Admiral. Mr. Henry Fuller, of Chicago, in his powerful novel, *The Cave Dwellers,* uses a still less elegant synonym for" scrap" — he talks of a "connubial spat." In the same book I note the phrases : " He teetered back and forth on his toes," " He was a stocky young man," " One of his brief noonings," " That's right, Claudia—score the profession." " Score," as used in America, does not mean "score off," but rather, I take it, "attack and leave your mark upon." It is very common in this sense. For instance, I note among the headlines of a New York paper, " Mr. So-and-so scores Yellow Journalism." Talking of Yellow Journalism, by the way, the expressions " a beat" and " a scoop " for what we in England call an " exclusive " item of news, were unknown to me until I went to America. I was a little bewildered, too, when I was told of a family which " lived on air-tights." Their diet consisted of canned (or, as we should say, tinned) provisions.

The most popular slang expression of the day is "to rubberneck," or, more concisely, "to rubber." Its primary meaning is to crane the neck in curiosity, to pry round the corner, as it were. [20] But it has

[19] Mr. Walkley reports that he has heard a Cockney policeman, speaking of a street row, say, " There's been a little scrappin'."

[20] "About a dozen ringers followed us into the church and stood around rubberin'." "Gettin' next to the new kinds o' saddles and rubberneckin to read the names on the tyres."—ARTIE. A writer in the New York Sun says: " I first heard the term rubber necks' in Arizona, about four years ago, applied to the throngs of onlookers in the gambling-houses, who strove to get a better view of the games in progress by stretching or bending their necks."

numerous and surprising extensions of meaning. It appears to be one of the laws of slang that when a phrase strikes the popular fancy, it is pressed into (service on every possible or impossible occasion. Another favourite expression is " That cuts no ice with me." [21] I was unable to ascertain either its origin or its precise signification. On the other hand, a piece of slang which supplies a "felt want," and will one day, I believe, pass into the literary language, is "the limit" in the sense of "le comble." A theatrical poster, widely displayed in New York while I was there, bore this alluring inscription:

"THE LIMIT AT LAST!
'THE MORMON SENATOR AND THE MERMAID.'
JAGS OF JOY FOR JADED JOHNNIES."

A "jag," be it known, means primarily a load, secondarily a " load " or " package " of alcohol.

Collectors of slang will find many priceless gems in two recent books which I commend to their notice : *Chimmie Fadden,* by Mr. E. W. Townsend, and *Artie,* by Mr. George Ade. *Chimmie Fadden* gives us the dialect of the New York Bowery Boy, or "tough," in which the most notable feature is the substitution either of " d " or " t " for " th." Is this,

[21] " We didn't break into sassiety notes, but that cuts no ice in our set"— ARTIE.

I wonder, a spontaneous corruption, or is it due to German and Yiddish influence? When Chimmie wants to express his admiration for a young lady, he says : " Well, say, she's a torrowbred, an' dat goes." When the young lady's father comes to thank him for championing her, this is how Chimmie describes the visit: "Den he gives me a song an' dance about me being a brave young man for tumping de mug what insulted his daughter." " Mug," the Bowery term for "fellow" or "man," in Chicago finds its equivalent in "guy." Mr. Ade's Artie is a Chicago clerk, and his dialect is of the most delectable. In comparison with him, Mr. Dooley is a well of English undefiled. Here again we find traces of the influence of polyglot immigration. " Ko-pecks " for "money " evidently comes from the Russian Jew; " girlerino," as a term of endearment, from the " Dago" of the sunny south; and " spiel," meaning practi-cally anything you please, from the Fatherland. When Artie goes to a wedding, he records that " there was a long spiel by the high guy in the pulpit." After describ-ing the embarrassments of a country cousin in the city, Artie proceeds, "Down at the farm, he was the wise guy and I was the soft mark." " Mark " in the sense of " butt" or " gull " is one of the commonest of slang words. When Artie has cut out all rivals in the good graces of his Mamie, he puts it thus, "There ain't nobody else in the one-two-sevens. They ain't even in the 'also rans.'" When they have a lovers' quarrel he remarks, " Well, I s'pose the other boy's fillin' all my dates." When he is asked whether Mamie cycles, he replies, " Does she ? She's a scorchalorum!" When he disapproves of another young gentleman, this is how " he puts him next " to the fact, as he himself would say—

" You're nothin, but a two-spot. You're the smallest thing in the deck… Chee-e-ese it! You can't do notion' like that to me and then come around afterwards and jolly me. Not in a million! I tell you you're a two-spot, and if you come into the same part o' the town with me I'll change your face. There's only one way to get back at you people…If he don't keep off o' my route, there'll be people walkin' slow behind him one o' these days…But this same two-spot's got a sister that can have my seat in the car any time she comes in."

I plead guilty to an unholy relish for Chimmie's and Artie's racy metaphors from the music-hall, the poker-table, and the "grip-car."[22] But it is to be noted that both these profound students of slang, Mr. Townsend and Mr. Ade, like the creator of the delightful Dooley, express themselves in pure and excellent Eng-lish the moment they drop the mask of their personage. This is very characteristic. Many educated Americans take great delight, and even pride, in keeping abreast of the daily developments of slang and patter; but this study does not in the

[22] Extract from a letter to the ***Chicago Evening Post:*** " I do not at all subscribe to the sneering remark of a talented author of my acquaintance,

to the effect that there were not enough cultured people in Chicago to fill a grip-car. I asked him if he meant a grip-car and a trailer, and he said, ' No; just one car.' And I told him right there that I could not agree with him."

least impair their sense for, or their command of, good English. The idea that the English language is degenerating in America is an absolutely groundless illusion. Take them all round, the newspapers of the leading American cities, in their editorial columns at any rate, are at least as well written as the newspapers of London; and in magazines and books the average level of literary accomplishment is certainly very high. There are bad and vulgar writers on both sides of the Atlantic; but until the beams are removed from our own eyes, we may safely trust the Americans to attend to the motes in theirs.

POSTSCRIPT.—When this paper originally appeared, it formed the text for an editorial article in the ***Daily News,*** in which Mr. Andrew Lang's sign manual was not to be mistaken. Mr. Lang brought my somewhat desultory discussion very neatly to a point. He admitted that we habitually use " Americanism " as a term of reproach; " but," he asked, " who is reproached ? Not the American (who may do as he pleases) but the English writer, who, in serious work, introduces, needlessly, an American phrase into our literature. We say ' needlessly' when our language already possesses a consecrated equivalent for the word or idiom."

In the first place, one has to remark that many English critics are far from accepting Mr. Lang's principle that " the American may do as he pleases, of course." Mr. Lang himself scarcely acts up to it in this very article. And, for my part, I think the principle a false one. I think the English language has been entrusted to the care of all of us, English no less than Americans, Americans no less than English ; and if I find an American writer debasing it in an essential point, as opposed to a point of mere local predilection, I assert my right to remonstrate with him, just as I admit his right, under similar circumstances, to remonstrate with me.

It is not here, however, that I join issue with Mr. Lang: it is on his theory that an English writer necessarily does wrong who unnecessarily employs an Americanism. This is a question of great practical moment, and I am glad that Mr. Lang has stated it in this definite form. My view is perhaps sufficiently indicated above, but I take the opportunity of re-asserting it with all deliberation. I believe that, as a matter both of literary and of social policy, we ought to encourage the free infiltration of graphic and racy Americanisms into our vernacular, and of vigorous and useful Americanisms (even if not absolutely necessary) into our literary language. Where is the harm in duplicating terms, if only the duplicates be in themselves good terms ? For instance, take the word "fall." Mr. Brander Matthews writes: " An American with a sense of the poetic cannot but prefer to the imported word 'autumn' the native and more logical word 'fall,' which the British have strangely suffered to drop into disuse." Well, " autumn " was a sufficiently early importation. "Our ancestors," wrote Lowell (quoted by Mr. Matthews in the same article), " unhappily could bring over no English better than Shakespeare's "; and in Shakespeare's (and Chaucer's) English they brought over "autumn." The word has inherent beauty as well as splendid poetical associations. I doubt whether even Shakespeare could have made out of " fall" so beautiful a line as

" The teeming autumn, big with rich increase."

I doubt whether Keats, had he written an **Ode to the Fall,** would have produced quite such a miraculous poem as that which begins.

" Season of mists and mellow fruitfulness."

Still, Mr. Matthews is quite right in saying that " fall" has a poetic value, a suggestion, an atmosphere of its own. I wonder, with him, why we dropped it, and I see no smallest reason why we should not recover it. The British literary patriotism which makes a point of never saying " fall" seems to me just as mistaken as the American literary patriotism (if such there be) that makes a merit of never saying " autumn." By insisting on such localisms (for the exclusive preference for either term is nothing more) we might, in process of time, bring about a serious fissure in the language. Of course there is no reason why Mr. Lang should force himself to use a word that is uncongenial to him; but if " fall" is congenial to me, I think I ought to be allowed to use it "without fear and without reproach."

Take, now, a colloquialism. How formal and colourless is the English phrase "I have enjoyed myself" beside the American "I have had a good time"! Each has its uses, no doubt. I am far from suggesting that the one should drive out the other. It is precisely the advantage of our linguistic position that it so enormously enlarges the stock of semi-synonyms at our disposal. To reject a forcible Americanism merely because we could, at a pinch, get on without it, is—Mr. Lang will understand the forcible Scotticism—to " sin our mercies."

Mr. Lang is under a certain illusion, I think, in his belief that in hardening our hearts against Americanisms we should raise no barrier between ourselves and the classical authors of America. He says : " Let us remark that they [Americanisms] do not occur in Hawthorne, Poe, Lowell, Longfellow, Prescott, and Emerson, except when these writers are consciously reproducing conversations in dialect." He made the same remark on a previous occasion ; when his opponent (see the *Academy* , March 30, 1895) opened a volume of Hawthorne and a volume of Emerson, and in five minutes found in Hawthorne " He had named his two children, one *for* Her Majesty and one *for* Prince Albert," and in Emerson " Nature tells every secret once. Yes; but in man she tells it *all the time*." The latter phrase is one which Mr. Lang explicitly puts under his ban. He is an ingenious and admirable translator : I wish he would translate Emerson's sentence from American into English, without loss of brevity, directness, and simple Saxon strength. For my part, I can think of nothing better than " In man she is always telling it," which strikes me as a feeble makeshift. "All the time," I suggest, is precisely one of the phrases we should accept with gratitude—if, indeed, it be not already naturalised.

Mr. Lang is peculiarly unfortunate in calling Oliver Wendell Holmes to witness against his particular and pet aversion "I belong here" or " That does not belong there." Writing of " needless Americanisms," he says, " The use of ' belong' as a new auxiliary verb [an odd classification, by the way] is an example of what we mean. Dr. Oliver Wendell Holmes was a stern opponent of such neologisms." I turn to the Oxford Dictionary, and the one quotation I find under "belong" in this sense, is—'"

You belong with the last set, and got accidentally shuffled with the others.'—O. W. *Holmes, 'Elsie Venner*.'" But this, Mr. Lang may say, is in dialogue. Yes, but not in *dialect.* I am very much mistaken if the locution does not occur elsewhere in Holmes. If Mr. Lang, in a leisure hour, were to undertake a search for it, he might incidentally find cause to modify his view as to the sternness of the Autocrat's anti-Americanism.

Let me not be thought to underrate the services which, by sound precept and invaluable example, Mr. Lang has rendered to all of us who use the English tongue. Conservatism and liberalism are as inevitable, nay, indispensable, in the world of words as in the world of deeds; and I trust Mr. Lang will not set down my liberalism as anarchism. He and I, in this little discussion, are simply playing our allotted parts. I believe (and Mr. Lang would probably admit with a shrug) that the forces of the future are on my side. May I recall to him that charming anecdote of Thackeray and Viscount Monck, when they were rival candidates for the . representation of Oxford in Parliament ? They met in the street one day, and exchanged a few words. On parting, Thackeray shook hands with his opponent and said, " Good-bye; and may the best man win!" "I hope not," replied Viscount Monck, with a bow. A hundred years hence, if some English-speaker of the future should chance to disinter this book from the recesses of the British Museum or the Library of Congress, and should read these final paragraphs, I doubt not he will say—for the immortal soul of the language even anarchism cannot affect—" the race is not always to the swift , nor the battle to the strong."

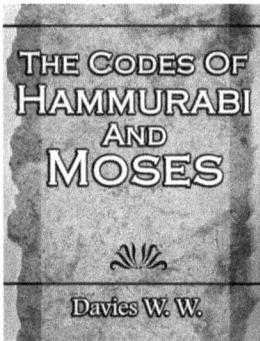

The Codes Of Hammurabi And Moses
W. W. Davies

QTY

The discovery of the Hammurabi Code is one of the greatest achievements of archaeology, and is of paramount interest, not only to the student of the Bible, but also to all those interested in ancient history...

Religion   ISBN: *1-59462-338-4*   **Pages:132**

MSRP $12.95

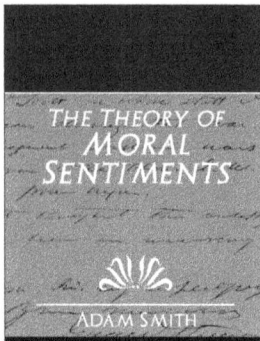

The Theory of Moral Sentiments
Adam Smith

QTY

This work from 1749. contains original theories of conscience amd moral judgment and it is the foundation for systemof morals.

Philosophy ISBN: *1-59462-777-0*   **Pages:536**

MSRP $19.95

Jessica's First Prayer
Hesba Stretton

QTY

In a screened and secluded corner of one of the many railway-bridges which span the streets of London there could be seen a few years ago, from five o'clock every morning until half past eight, a tidily set-out coffee-stall, consisting of a trestle and board, upon which stood two large tin cans, with a small fire of charcoal burning under each so as to keep the coffee boiling during the early hours of the morning when the work-people were thronging into the city on their way to their daily toil...

Pages:84

Childrens   ISBN: *1-59462-373-2*   *MSRP $9.95*

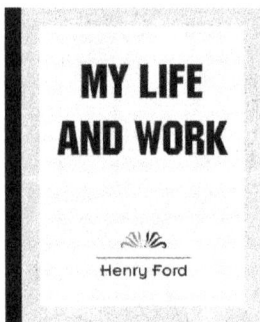

My Life and Work
Henry Ford

QTY

Henry Ford revolutionized the world with his implementation of mass production for the Model T automobile. Gain valuable business insight into his life and work with his own auto-biography... "We have only started on our development of our country we have not as yet, with all our talk of wonderful progress, done more than scratch the surface. The progress has been wonderful enough but..."

Pages:300

Biographies/   ISBN: *1-59462-198-5*   *MSRP $21.95*

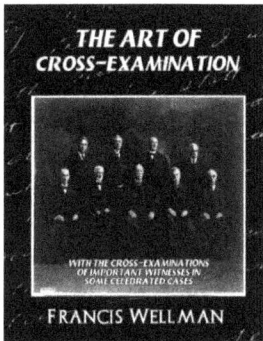

The Art of Cross-Examination
Francis Wellman

QTY

I presume it is the experience of every author, after his first book is published upon an important subject, to be almost overwhelmed with a wealth of ideas and illustrations which could readily have been included in his book, and which to his own mind, at least, seem to make a second edition inevitable. Such certainly was the case with me; and when the first edition had reached its sixth impression in five months, I rejoiced to learn that it seemed to my publishers that the book had met with a sufficiently favorable reception to justify a second and considerably enlarged edition. ..

Pages:412

Reference **ISBN: *1-59462-647-2*** *MSRP $19.95*

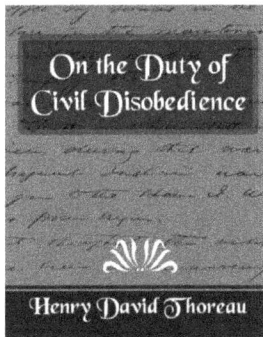

On the Duty of Civil Disobedience
Henry David Thoreau

QTY

Thoreau wrote his famous essay, On the Duty of Civil Disobedience, as a protest against an unjust but popular war and the immoral but popular institution of slave-owning. He did more than write—he declined to pay his taxes, and was hauled off to gaol in consequence. Who can say how much this refusal of his hastened the end of the war and of slavery ?

Law **ISBN: *1-59462-747-9*** **Pages:48**

MSRP $7.45

Dream Psychology Psychoanalysis for Beginners
Sigmund Freud

QTY

Sigmund Freud, born Sigismund Schlomo Freud (May 6, 1856 - September 23, 1939), was a Jewish-Austrian neurologist and psychiatrist who co-founded the psychoanalytic school of psychology. Freud is best known for his theories of the unconscious mind, especially involving the mechanism of repression; his redefinition of sexual desire as mobile and directed towards a wide variety of objects; and his therapeutic techniques, especially his understanding of transference in the therapeutic relationship and the presumed value of dreams as sources of insight into unconscious desires.

Pages:196

Psychology **ISBN: *1-59462-905-6*** *MSRP $15.45*

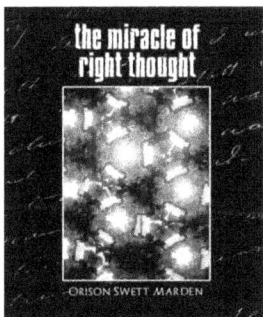

The Miracle of Right Thought
Orison Swett Marden

QTY

Believe with all of your heart that you will do what you were made to do. When the mind has once formed the habit of holding cheerful, happy, prosperous pictures, it will not be easy to form the opposite habit. It does not matter how improbable or how far away this realization may see, or how dark the prospects may be, if we visualize them as best we can, as vividly as possible, hold tenaciously to them and vigorously struggle to attain them, they will gradually become actualized, realized in the life. But a desire, a longing without endeavor, a yearning abandoned or held indifferently will vanish without realization.

Pages:360

Self Help **ISBN: *1-59462-644-8*** *MSRP $25.45*

The Rosicrucian Cosmo-Conception Mystic Christianity *by Max Heindel* ISBN: *1-59462-188-8* **$38.95**
The Rosicrucian Cosmo-conception is not dogmatic, neither does it appeal to any other authority than the reason of the student. It is: not controversial, but is: sent forth in the, hope that it may help to clear... New Age/Religion Pages 646

Abandonment To Divine Providence *by Jean-Pierre de Caussade* ISBN: *1-59462-228-0* **$25.95**
"The Rev. Jean Pierre de Caussade was one of the most remarkable spiritual writers of the Society of Jesus in France in the 18th Century. His death took place at Toulouse in 1751. His works have gone through many editions and have been republished... Inspirational/Religion Pages 400

Mental Chemistry *by Charles Haanel* ISBN: *1-59462-192-6* **$23.95**
Mental Chemistry allows the change of material conditions by combining and appropriately utilizing the power of the mind. Much like applied chemistry creates something new and unique out of careful combinations of chemicals the mastery of mental chemistry... New Age Pages 354

The Letters of Robert Browning and Elizabeth Barret Barrett 1845-1846 vol II ISBN: *1-59462-193-4* **$35.95**
by Robert Browning and Elizabeth Barrett Biographies Pages 596

Gleanings In Genesis (volume I) *by Arthur W. Pink* ISBN: *1-59462-130-6* **$27.45**
Appropriately has Genesis been termed "the seed plot of the Bible" for in it we have, in germ form, almost all of the great doctrines which are afterwards fully developed in the books of Scripture which follow... Religion/Inspirational Pages 420

The Master Key *by L. W. de Laurence* ISBN: *1-59462-001-6* **$30.95**
In no branch of human knowledge has there been a more lively increase of the spirit of research during the past few years than in the study of Psychology, Concentration and Mental Discipline. The requests for authentic lessons in Thought Control, Mental Discipline and... New Age/Business Pages 422

The Lesser Key Of Solomon Goetia *by L. W. de Laurence* ISBN: *1-59462-092-X* **$9.95**
This translation of the first book of the "Lernegton" which is now for the first time made accessible to students of Talismanic Magic was done, after careful collation and edition, from numerous Ancient Manuscripts in Hebrew, Latin, and French... New Age/Occult Pages 92

Rubaiyat Of Omar Khayyam *by Edward Fitzgerald* ISBN:*1-59462-332-5* **$13.95**
Edward Fitzgerald, whom the world has already learned, in spite of his own efforts to remain within the shadow of anonymity, to look upon as one of the rarest poets of the century, was born at Bredfield, in Suffolk, on the 31st of March, 1809. He was the third son of John Purcell... Music Pages 172

Ancient Law *by Henry Maine* ISBN: *1-59462-128-4* **$29.95**
The chief object of the following pages is to indicate some of the earliest ideas of mankind, as they are reflected in Ancient Law, and to point out the relation of those ideas to modern thought. Religiom/History Pages 452

Far-Away Stories *by William J. Locke* ISBN: *1-59462-129-2* **$19.45**
"Good wine needs no bush, but a collection of mixed vintages does. And this book is just such a collection. Some of the stories I do not want to remain buried for ever in the museum files of dead magazine-numbers an author's not unpardonable vanity..." Fiction Pages 272

Life of David Crockett *by David Crockett* ISBN: *1-59462-250-7* **$27.45**
"Colonel David Crockett was one of the most remarkable men of the times in which he lived. Born in humble life, but gifted with a strong will, an indomitable courage, and unremitting perseverance... Biographies/New Age Pages 424

Lip-Reading *by Edward Nitchie* ISBN: *1-59462-206-X* **$25.95**
Edward B. Nitchie, founder of the New York School for the Hard of Hearing, now the Nitchie School of Lip-Reading, Inc, wrote "LIP-READING Principles and Practice". The development and perfecting of this meritorious work on lip-reading was an undertaking... How-to Pages 400

A Handbook of Suggestive Therapeutics, Applied Hypnotism, Psychic Science ISBN: *1-59462-214-0* **$24.95**
by Henry Munro Health/New Age/Health/Self-help Pages 376

A Doll's House: and Two Other Plays *by Henrik Ibsen* ISBN: *1-59462-112-8* **$19.95**
Henrik Ibsen created this classic when in revolutionary 1848 Rome. Introducing some striking concepts in playwriting for the realist genre, this play has been studied the world over. Fiction/Classics/Plays 308

The Light of Asia *by sir Edwin Arnold* ISBN: *1-59462-204-3* **$13.95**
In this poetic masterpiece, Edwin Arnold describes the life and teachings of Buddha. The man who was to become known as Buddha to the world was born as Prince Gautama of India but he rejected the worldly riches and abandoned the reigns of power when... Religion/History/Biographies Pages 170

The Complete Works of Guy de Maupassant *by Guy de Maupassant* ISBN: *1-59462-157-8* **$16.95**
"For days and days, nights and nights, I had dreamed of that first kiss which was to consecrate our engagement, and I knew not on what spot I should put my lips..." Fiction/Classics Pages 240

The Art of Cross-Examination *by Francis L. Wellman* ISBN: *1-59462-309-0* **$26.95**
Written by a renowned trial lawyer, Wellman imparts his experience and uses case studies to explain how to use psychology to extract desired information through questioning. How-to/Science/Reference Pages 408

Answered or Unanswered? *by Louisa Vaughan* ISBN: *1-59462-248-5* **$10.95**
Miracles of Faith in China Religion Pages 112

The Edinburgh Lectures on Mental Science (1909) *by Thomas* ISBN: *1-59462-008-3* **$11.95**
This book contains the substance of a course of lectures recently given by the writer in the Queen Street Hail, Edinburgh. Its purpose is to indicate the Natural Principles governing the relation between Mental Action and Material Conditions... New Age/Psychology Pages 148

Ayesha *by H. Rider Haggard* ISBN: *1-59462-301-5* **$24.95**
Verily and indeed it is the unexpected that happens! Probably if there was one person upon the earth from whom the Editor of this, and of a certain previous history, did not expect to hear again... Classics Pages 380

Ayala's Angel *by Anthony Trollope* ISBN: *1-59462-352-X* **$29.95**
The two girls were both pretty, but Lucy who was twenty-one who supposed to be simple and comparatively unattractive, whereas Ayala was credited, as her Bombwhat romantic name might show, with poetic charm and a taste for romance. Ayala when her father died was nineteen... Fiction Pages 484

The American Commonwealth *by James Bryce* ISBN: *1-59462-286-8* **$34.45**
An interpretation of American democratic political theory. It examines political mechanics and society from the perspective of Scotsman James Bryce Politics Pages 572

Stories of the Pilgrims *by Margaret P. Pumphrey* ISBN: *1-59462-116-0* **$17.95**
This book explores pilgrims religious oppression in England as well as their escape to Holland and eventual crossing to America on the Mayflower, and their early days in New England... History Pages 268

www.bookjungle.com *email: sales@bookjungle.com fax: 630-214-0564 mail: Book Jungle PO Box 2226 Champaign, IL 61825*

QTY

The Fasting Cure *by Sinclair Upton*   ISBN: *1-59462-222-1* **$13.95**
*In the Cosmopolitan Magazine for May, 1910, and in the Contemporary Review (London) for April, 1910, I published an article dealing with my experi-
ences in fasting. I have written a great many magazine articles, but never one which attracted so much attention...* New Age/Self Help/Health Pages 164

Hebrew Astrology *by Sepharial*   ISBN: *1-59462-308-2* **$13.45**
*In these days of advanced thinking it is a matter of common observation that we have left many of the old landmarks behind and that we are now pressing
forward to greater heights and to a wider horizon than that which represented the mind-content of our progenitors...* Astrology Pages 144

Thought Vibration or The Law of Attraction in the Thought World   ISBN: *1-59462-127-6* **$12.95**
by William Walker Atkinson   Psychology/Religion Pages 144

Optimism *by Helen Keller*   ISBN: *1-59462-108-X* **$15.95**
*Helen Keller was blind, deaf, and mute since 19 months old, yet famously learned how to overcome these handicaps, communicate with the world, and
spread her lectures promoting optimism. An inspiring read for everyone...* Biographies/Inspirational Pages 84

Sara Crewe *by Frances Burnett*   ISBN: *1-59462-360-0* **$9.45**
*In the first place, Miss Minchin lived in London. Her home was a large, dull, tall one, in a large, dull square, where all the houses were alike, and all the
sparrows were alike, and where all the door-knockers made the same heavy sound...* Childrens/Classic Pages 88

The Autobiography of Benjamin Franklin *by Benjamin Franklin*   ISBN: *1-59462-135-7* **$24.95**
*The Autobiography of Benjamin Franklin has probably been more extensively read than any other American historical work, and no other book of its kind
has had such ups and downs of fortune. Franklin lived for many years in England, where he was agent...* Biographies/History Pages 332

Name	
Email	
Telephone	
Address	
City, State ZIP	

☐ **Credit Card**   ☐ **Check / Money Order**

Credit Card Number	
Expiration Date	
Signature	

*Please Mail to: Book Jungle
PO Box 2226
Champaign, IL 61825
or Fax to: 630-214-0564*

ORDERING INFORMATION

web*: www.bookjungle.com*
email*: sales@bookjungle.com*
fax*: 630-214-0564*
mail*: Book Jungle PO Box 2226 Champaign, IL 61825*
or PayPal *to sales@bookjungle.com*

Please contact us for bulk discounts

DIRECT-ORDER TERMS

**20% Discount if You Order
Two or More Books**
Free Domestic Shipping!
Accepted: Master Card, Visa,
Discover, American Express

www.ingramcontent.com/pod-product-compliance
Lightning Source LLC
Chambersburg PA
CBHW081231090426
42738CB00016B/3257